# How to Introduce Your Jewish Friends to the Messiah

# How to Introduce Your Jewish Friends to the Messiah

**Chosen People Ministries**
**241 East 51st Street**
**New York, NY 10022**
**212-223-2252**

**Chosen People Ministries (Canada)**
**P.O. Box 897 Sta B**
**North York ON M2K 2R1**

**HOW TO INTRODUCE YOUR JEWISH FRIENDS TO THE MESSIAH.**

Published and distributed by Chosen People Ministries, Inc., P.O. Box 195003, Charlotte, NC 28219-5003. (704) 357-9000.
In Canada: CPM (Canada), P.O. Box 897 Station B, North York, ON M2K 2R1, CANADA. (416) 250-0177.
In Israel: Beit Sar Shalom, Box 637, Kfar Saba, ISRAEL. 011-972-9-958-256.

**ISBN  1-882675-00-2**

Printed in the United States of America

# Contents

# Preface

This revised and expanded edition of our first witnessing booklet, *Introducing the Jewish People to Their Messiah*, is not only published under a new title—*How to Introduce Your Jewish Friends to the Messiah*—but it contains additional information on witnessing techniques, Jewish history, current attitudes toward anti-Semitism and Israel, Jewish terminology, and updated bibliographic materials.

Our grateful appreciation is extended to the many staff workers of Chosen People Ministries (CPM) who have contributed materials and ideas that have helped make this book possible, useable, and practical.

A special thanks is extended to Ruth Fleischer Snow, a former CPM staff worker, who, several years ago, edited, wrote, and rewrote much of the material for the first edition, *Introducing the Jewish People to Their Messiah*.

It is our prayer that this new and revised edition will encourage even more Christians to share their faith with their Jewish friends, thereby helping extend even further our Gospel witness to the Jewish people.

—Chosen People Ministries

# Preface to the First Edition

This manual is the result of many contributions on the part of Chosen People Ministries' missionaries who labor daily to bring the Good News of Yeshua haMeshiach (Jesus the Christ) to His chosen people.

It is our prayer that its use will redound to the glory of God because faithful Christians have responded to our Lord's words: "... I have chosen you, and ordained you, that ye should go and bring forth fruit, and that your fruit should remain" (John 15:16).

We often find it difficult to share the Gospel with those whom we do not know well or feel we do not understand. If we are confused about the needs of a particular people, it is especially awkward to attempt to witness to them about our faith. For many people, an outreach to Jewish friends and neighbors is undertaken with trepidation and uncertainty born of ignorance and misinformation.

It is our hope that this manual will help to erase those misunderstandings and guide those who really desire to reach Jewish people with the message of salvation. The blessings that await you as you share your faith will return to you a hundred fold. God promises: "I will bless them that bless thee, and curse him that curseth thee: and in thee shall all families of the earth be blessed" (Genesis 12:3).

# Why Witness?

In the New Covenant, the followers of Yeshua are commissioned with these words: "Go ye therefore, and teach all nations..." (Matthew 28:19).

The first men to whom these words were addressed were all Jews. It was their special ministry to take the Good News, not only to their own people, but to the nations—to the Gentiles. And they faithfully fulfilled the Lord's commission.

But all too frequently Gentiles have neglected to reciprocate— and still do—the favor done them by these early Jewish believers. Even though the Gentiles were excluded from the Gospel at its inception, God later made it clear that they did not have to become Jews before they could accept Jesus!

## A CHALLENGE: WHY WITNESS TO THE JEWISH PEOPLE?

1. We are commanded to take the Good News of Messiah's atonement to all peoples (Matthew 28:18-20).
2. According to Romans 1:16, the Gospel is "to the Jew first."
3. God's love for Israel is demonstrated throughout Scripture. As His children, we should have a love for His chosen people and desire their reconciliation with God through His Son (Romans 9–11).
4. All believers owe a great debt of love to the Jewish people, as we see in Romans 11. Our faith came to us through them:
   a. The Holy Scriptures were written by Jews under inspiration of the Holy Spirit.

1

b. God revealed Himself as the God of Israel.

c. Yeshua was born of a Jewish mother not by accident but as a condition of His birth (Genesis 49:10; Psalm 132:11; Micah 5:2).

d. The roots of our faith are the concepts of Old Testament Jewish theology, such as the need for a blood atonement (Leviticus 17:11).

e. Every believer looks toward the Messiah's eternal reign, which was specifically promised to King David as part of the Davidic Covenant (2 Samuel 7:16).

f. It is the direct intention of God that the Gentiles who believe in Yeshua should, by their lives, provoke the Jewish people to jealousy (Romans 11:11-15).

# Our Purpose

We are desirous of sharing our faith with Jewish friends and neighbors. Such sharing must be done wisely if it is to be effective. We should always remember that the faith we are sharing *originated* with Jews. Jewish people who accept Yeshua as their Messiah do not "convert to another religion" but actually return to the faith of Abraham, Isaac, and Jacob fulfilled!

The purpose of this manual is to provide believers with the necessary information and understanding so that they will be able to present the Lord they love and serve to Jewish friends and neighbors in the very best possible way. Studying these notes will not make you an expert, but it will equip you with some of the most essential tools. Added to your *love* and *concern* for the Jewish people and the power of the Holy Spirit, this knowledge should enable you to share the Messiah with Jewish people.

## DEFINING TERMS

In the course of this material, we use certain words that may convey a different meaning to you than the one we intend. Following is a list of these terms and the definitions we want you to keep in mind as you read the remainder of this manual:

**Yeshua**—Hebrew name for Jesus, meaning Savior
**Meshiach**—Hebrew for *Messiah,* meaning "the Anointed One" (expressed in the Greek as "Christos" or "Christ")
**Brit haDasha**—New Covenant or New Testament
**Messiah**—Savior, Lord, Redeemer, Christ

**Believer**— "Christian," one who truly trusts in Jesus as Messiah and Son of God.

**Fulfilled** or **Completed**—Said of a Jewish person who accepts Jesus as his personal Messiah and Savior. Jewish people will readily recognize the meaning you are giving to these words and will be less defensive about what you are really trying to communicate. It is a good idea to get into the habit of *thinking* in these terms. This is why they are used here (*see* "Do's and Don'ts of Terminology").

# Understanding
# Jewish People

"And unto the Jews I became as a Jew, that I might gain the Jews....I am made all things to all men, that I might by all means save some" (1 Corinthians 9:20-22).

## MISCONCEPTIONS: GENTILE AND JEWISH

There are many misconceptions among Gentiles in regard to Jews, and among Jews in regard to Gentiles. It is important for you to identify and deal with them if you are to share in a sensitive manner.

### Common Gentile Misconceptions

*All Jews look alike and think alike.* Actually, there are blue-eyed, blond Jews as well as brown-eyed, olive-skinned brunettes. Many Jewish people are more politically and socially liberal, but many are also conservative. Some Jews are Orthodox or Chasidic, but the majority of American Jews are agnostic or secular; few Jews know or even read the Old Testament.

*All Jewish people are wealthy.* Many Jews are very hardworking and industrious, but they are not the big moneymakers. Of the 50 wealthiest families in the United States, not one is Jewish; of the 400 richest U.S. families, only 10 percent (40 families) are Jewish.

*Jews do not believe in Jesus.* All of the Messiah's early followers and disciples were Jewish, and the New Testament declares that "the common people [the Jews] heard him gladly" (Mark 12:37b). The leaders were jealous of Jesus' popularity and eventually convinced Pilate to have Him executed. But the Romans actually made the decision to kill Him, and He was executed by them. Although the majority of Jewish people today do not believe that Jesus is the promised Messiah, many Jews are accepting Him!

*Jewish people are stingy.* The Western literary tradition has produced innumerable stereotypes (such as "Shylock" in *The Merchant of Venice* or "Fagin" in *Oliver Twist*). These stereotypes define all Jewish people as "cheap" and "stingy." In fact, however, Jews contribute large sums to charities of every type. They are often involved in worthy causes. In many cases they are exceptionally generous with whatever they have. At worst, Jews are not much different from anyone else. We should appreciate Jewish contributions to the world and be particularly thankful for all that is ours because of the Jewish people (*see* "A Challenge: Why Witness to the Jewish People?").

## Common Jewish Misconceptions

*All Gentiles are Christians.* Hitler, the Pope, the minister of your church, Billy Graham, and Queen Elizabeth are categorized in this way. A true Christian (a real believer) is a follower of Yeshua and is not merely a church member. Yeshua said, "If a man loves me, he will keep my words; and my Father will love him, and we will come unto him, and make our abode with him. He that loveth me not keepeth not my sayings; and the word which ye hear is not mine, but the Father's, who sent me" (John 14:23, 24). Only those who have accepted Him as their Messiah and seek to do as He commands are really Christians, according to the Bible.

*Christians are all anti-Semites.* People who are *true followers* of the Messiah *cannot* hate anyone, but they seek the well-being of all: "He that loveth not knoweth not God; for God is love" (1 John 4:8).

*Christians worship three gods.* Actually, Christians believe in only one God—the God of the Bible, the God of Abraham, Isaac, and Jacob. A true Christian believes that God has a unique unity (*see* "An Explanation of Jewish Objections").

*Christians are pro-Arab.* True Christians realize that the Bible also teaches that God has a place and a plan for the Arabs, the descendants of Hagar, in His program of redemption. True Christians also believe that the Bible teaches that God chose the Jewish people and gave them the land (Genesis 13:14-17), that He promised to restore and regather the Jewish people, and that this prophecy is fulfilled in the nation of Israel (Jeremiah 16:14, 15). Christians should love Israel because of God's love, but they should also be concerned for the plight of the Arabs, who fail to recognize God's hand in the Jewish state. True believers "pray for the peace of Jerusalem" (Psalm 122:6-9) regularly (*see* "Prophecy Concerning Israel").

## JEWISH RELIGIOUS SENSITIVITIES

Jewish people have experienced thousands of years of persecution. They are sensitive about their cultural and religious practices, their life styles, and so forth. Who is not? Some typical religious sensitivities are as follows:

*Exclusiveness of Salvation:* Jewish religious sensitivities often center around the exclusiveness of salvation, which is available only to those who accept Yeshua as their Savior. Although Chasidic, Orthodox, and some Conservative Jews do believe in one way to God—through *Mitzvah*, *Torah*, and *Talmud*—this way is only available to Jews. The Bible teaches only one way for all mankind—through Yeshua (John 14:6).

*The Miraculous:* Conservative, Reform, or secular Jews find it difficult to believe in Biblical inspiration or in a literal interpretation of the Scriptures (*see* "Judaism Today"). Thus, any miraculous event is questionable to them, for example, Messiah's virgin birth, deity, resurrection, ascension, and so forth.

*Traitors to Their People:* Jewish people have been taught to believe that they are traitors to their people if they accept Yeshua as Messiah. They feel that such an act discounts all the Jewish blood that has been shed and all the Jewish lives that have been lost in pogroms, inquisitions, and gas chambers.

## JEWISH CULTURAL SIMILARITIES

Culturally Jews may vary, but they share certain similarities. For instance,

*Most Jewish people are educationally minded:* Coupled with this is an independence of thought and action. Jews are often amazed at the lack of independent thinking in Christian circles.

*Jewish people are usually very "definite":* They often wholeheartedly support any cause they believe in with all their energies. Because they are open and sincere, they often dislike and resent subterfuge.

*Jewish people love peace:* They are taught to love peace but will fiercely defend themselves if necessary. As Golda Meir put it, "We can forgive you for killing our sons, but we cannot forgive you for forcing us to kill yours."

*Jewish people love Israel:* The majority of Jews share one common interest—the State of Israel. They see Israel as the Jewish homeland, even though they may never live there. Jewish people are particularly sensitive to criticism of Israel or any negative attitudes toward it (*see* "Judaism Today"; "Prophecy Concerning Israel").

*Jewish people are sensitive to criticism of Jewish leaders and organizations:* All people resent negative remarks about their "families."

## DO'S AND DON'TS OF TERMINOLOGY

Certain words or expressions are particularly offensive to Jewish people. If you desire to be an effective witness, avoid using them. Instead, learn to use words and expressions with more positive connotations.

**DON'T SAY** "Christian." **DO SAY** "Believer." To the average Jew, the term *Christian* means any Gentile, a term that includes Catholics, Protestants, true believers, and nominal church members.

**DON'T SAY** "Christ." **DO SAY** "Messiah" or "Yeshua haMeshiach" for Jesus, the Christ. To the Jewish mind, "Christ"

is the god of the Gentiles and the name in which Jews have been persecuted for almost two thousand years. *Messiah* is a Hebrew word meaning "Anointed One." It has the same meaning as *Christ,* which is a Greek word. Also, the Messianic idea is a familiar concept in Judaism, but remember that the Jewish concept of the Messiah differs from ours.

**DON'T SAY** "Convert." **DO SAY** "Completed" or "Fulfilled." Such terms as *saved* and *born again* are meaningless to unbelievers. "Conversion" is the thing most feared by Jewish people. Pagans may "convert," but Jews really return to the faith of Abraham fulfilled in the Messiah (Hebrews 11:8-16).

**DON'T SAY** "Cross." **DO SAY** "Tree." The cross has been a sign under which much persecution of Jewish people has taken place. It is also better to avoid display of a cross.

**DON'T SAY** "Old Testament" and "New Testament." **DO SAY** "Old Covenant" and "New Covenant." Jewish people refer to the Old Testament as the Bible or the "Tenach" and to the Books of Moses as the "Torah" (Law). The New Testament is considered a non-Jewish book, so it is better to *use* the book without placing emphasis on its name. Do be certain to emphasize the Jewishness of its writers. When possible, use "Holy Scriptures" or "Bible" for any reference.

**DON'T SAY** "Church." **DO SAY** "Congregation." Today the word *church* carries with it a Gentile connotation (and thus a negative one) to many Jewish people.

As you can see, our choice of vocabulary can be important. Here are a few additional guidelines:

■ When communicating New Covenant truth, emphasize the Jewishness of the early congregation.

■ When describing Jewish people who believe in Jesus, speak of them as *Messianic Jews* or *Biblical Jews* rather than as *Hebrew Christians* or *Jewish Christians.*

■ When speaking of the places of worship for Messianic Jews, refer to them as *Messianic congregations* or by the name of the congregation rather than as *Messianic synagogues.*

■ When referring to the spiritual leaders of Messianic congregations, use terms such as *rabbi, pastors, teachers, elders. Do not* refer to them as *cantors* and so forth. Using terms such as *synagogue, cantor,* and so forth, when used by or of Messianic believers, can lead to a charge of deception by the Jewish community. It is better not to use any of these terms, as they can lead to confusion and to a poor testimony.

## AN HISTORICAL OVERVIEW

In order to understand the Jewish problem in accepting Yeshua as the Messiah, it is necessary to have some knowledge of the Jewish experience with "Christianity." From an historical perspective, religious anti-Semitism has been the major deterrent in sharing the Gospel with Jewish people. Once this factor is understood, much can be done to overcome Jewish resistance and fear.

Jerusalem was the center of belief in Yeshua—Christianity was at first considered a sect of Judaism—until A.D. 70, when Jerusalem was destroyed by Titus and the Diaspora began in earnest. At that time, and after the last Jewish struggle for independence in A.D. 130-135, the Jewish people (including believers) were dispersed, and Rome became the center of the faith.

As the Gospel spread throughout the Gentile world, the majority of believers were no longer Jewish. Emphasis shifted from the Jewish to the Gentile, and the promised Jewish Messiah, Yeshua, became the Greco-Roman Savior, Jesus Christ. Yeshua was "removed" historically and culturally from His Jewish setting, taking on the trappings of whatever society His message was being preached in.

From the original premise—that only Jews could be followers of the Messiah—the trend of the organized Church based in the Roman world was to suggest that Jews—*as such—could not* be followers of *their* Christ! Even the New Covenant, which had been written by Jews, was used to support this anti-Jewish thesis.

Unfortunately, leading members of the Church hierarchy encouraged anti-Semitism, as did secular leaders. For example, Justin Martyr accused the Jews of inciting Romans to kill Christians after having murdered God (*Nicene Fathers*, Vol. I, chap. 16:5, pp. 202, 203), although Yeshua said, "I lay down my life, that I may take it up again. No man taketh it from me" (John 10:17, 18).

After A.D. 130-135, Gentile believers sought to divorce themselves from the Jewish people because of the Jewish uprising against Rome. Any Church practice that had Jewish roots was replaced with a practice having Gentile roots. For example, Passover, which had been kept by *all* believers as a memorial of Yeshua's sacrifice, was altered. First, the date was changed so that it would not correspond with the Jewish Passover; then the name was changed to Easter (named after a pagan goddess), and the Biblical "remembrance" became the completely unscriptural "mass."

Jerome (A.D. 340-419), originator of the Latin Vulgate, although taught by a scholarly Jewish rabbi, followed the pattern set by Augustine: "God hates the Jews, and I hate the Jews" (Philip Schaff *History of the Christian Church*, Vol. III, pp. 970, 971). Yet in the book of Jeremiah, God declares, "Yea, I have loved thee with an everlasting love: therefore with lovingkindness I have drawn thee" (Jeremiah 31:3, 4).

Chrysostom, Patriarch of Constantinople (A.D. 344-407), said, "Jews are the most worthless of men—they are lecherous, greedy, rapacious . . . they worship the devil. It is incumbent on all Christians to hate Jews" (*Homily* 1:3-6; 4:1).

Of Cyril, Patriarch of Alexandria, it is written, "In the year 415 he fell upon the synagogues of the very numerous Jews with armed force. . . . he put some to death and drove out the rest, and exposed their property to the excited multitude" (Philip Schaff, *History of the Christian Church,* Vol. III, pp. 942, 943).

Clovis, chieftain of the Franks (A.D. 481-511), was converted to

Catholicism. He declared that if he had been present at the crucifixion, he and his Franks would have killed the Jews in order to save Yeshua. None of the Church leaders clarified the necessity of Yeshua's death in atonement for sins.

Richard of England, known as "Lion-hearted," expelled the Jews from his nation in 1189 and confiscated their property.

Thomas Aquinas, the foremost scholasticist and Church authority of the Medieval Period, wrote in 1247, "It would be perfectly licit to hold the Jews, because of their crucifying our Lord, in perpetual servitude" (Dagobert Runes, *The Jew and the Cross,* p. 41).

The Crusades were organized, not as pious undertakings for the cause of God, which we have been led to believe by Hollywood, but as a proposed means to gain wealth, land, honor, and glory. Along the way,

■ At Rouen, all Jews unwilling to submit to baptism were put to death.

■ At Worms, Jews were massacred and their property divided among the murderers.

■ At Jerusalem, in 1099, the Great Synagogue was burned to the ground with all the Jews of the city inside, while the perpetrators of this mass murder marched around the synagogue chanting hymns.

In the Middle Ages, Jews were charged with sorcery and were blamed for epidemics such as the Black Plague, for natural disasters such as the massive Lisbon earthquake, and for other unexplained catastrophes. They were even charged with the ritual murder of Christian children who were supposedly killed so that their blood could be used to make matzot for Passover.

The Roman Catholic Church, which dominated Europe, held Jews *of all times* responsible for the death of Yeshua, although His death is an essential part of Church dogma and despite Yeshua's own statement (John 10:17, 18). This doctrine was officially nullified only a few years ago.

The Inquisitions of fifteenth-century Spain and Portugal were attempts by the state church to legislate conformity. Jews were forced to embrace Catholicism or leave their homes and all their belongings for unknown and probably unfriendly lands. Those Jews who "converted" were subject to harassment and even death on the slimmest evidence that they were "secret" Jews.

Martin Luther, the leading Protestant reformer of the sixteenth century, at first had a deep regard for Jewish people. However, when they did not flock to his banner, he came to resent them. He supported his resentment with the theology that Jews had been rejected by God and *could not be saved!* In one of his last sermons, Luther declared, "If the Jews refuse to be converted, we ought not to suffer them or bear with them any longer."

During the seventeenth century Jews were expelled from Frankfurt, Prague, and Vienna as well as from numerous towns and villages. Pogroms, mass murder, and vandalism of Jewish people in Russia and Poland in the eighteenth, nineteenth, and early twentieth centuries were instigated by the state church; by the state itself; and, in particular, by local clergymen. The most terrible pogrom took place in Kishinev in 1905.

The Dreyfus Affair in the 1890s took place in a nation praised for its enlightenment and liberalism. Captain Alfred Dreyfus, a Jew, was accused of selling military secrets to the Prussians. No proof existed to support this charge, but he was found guilty and sent to the horrible prison at Devil's Island. During his trial it was insinuated that Jews could not be trusted, that they were alien to France because they were not "Christian." Mass hysteria and mob violence, often encouraged by clergymen, shook Marseilles and other French cities and towns; Jews were beaten and murdered, their property confiscated or destroyed.

Eventually, through the work of Emile Zola and others, Dreyfus was proved innocent and high army officials were implicated in the original treachery as well as in the false accusation and cover-up that followed. But anti-Jewish feelings persisted.

Theodore Herzl, a young Austrian Jewish journalist who witnessed the Dreyfus Affair, abandoned his view that Jewish assimilation was the solution to anti-Semitism. He wrote *Der Juden Stat,* supporting the idea of a Jewish national homeland.

The Holocaust of the late 1930s and early 1940s took place in Germany, a so-called Christian country and the home of some of the most outstanding and respected theologians. For instance, in 1943, the Jews of Nuremberg were assembled and burned "for the greater glory of Christ." The nations of the world watched as the Third Reich slaughtered six million Jews, refusing refuge and safety to Jewish refugees fleeing death.

> *How odd of God*
> *To choose the Jews,*
> *But odder still*
> *To choose the Jewish God,*
> *And shun the Jews.*
> *—Anonymous*

## Anti-Semitism in Literature

The image of Jewish people in Europe and America, from the Dispersion to the present, has remained relatively unchanged in literature. Jews are pictured as evil, ignoble, and corrupt—as being outside society. Examples of this stereotype are seen in literary works by such great writers as Geoffrey Chaucer, William Shakespeare, Christopher Marlowe, Charles Dickens, Sir Walter Scott, Thomas Wolfe, and others.

Early in the twentieth century, the *Protocols of the Learned Elders of Zion,* which was originally a play written for the "amusement" of Russian Tsar Nicholas II and later published in booklet form, began to be accepted as factual information regarding the planned takeover of the "Christian" world by Jews. It has been widely circulated and is still read and believed today.

Since 1917 claims have been made that Russian Communism (as well as American Imperialism) is part of this insidious Judaistic, Talmudic plot. In a clarification to the 1930 edition of the *Protocols,* the editor declared, "The author is not against Jews as 'Jews,' as individuals or as a religion; but is anti-Jewish solely because their leadership is actively anti-American, and because the Jewish people refuse to repudiate it" (p. 68).

*The Cross and the Flag* and other such publications continue to encourage anti-Semitism in the name of Christianity. Men such as Gerald L. K. Smith and Gerald Winrod have promoted hatred of Jews while declaring that they were serving God. In a recently reprinted article entitled, "Are You an Anti-Semite?" anti-Semitism was equated with patriotism and Christianity (published by the Keep America Christian Committee).

Today, anti-Semitism along with hatred of Israel is growing. Such neo-Nazi groups as the Skinheads and the Aryan Nations continue to stir up hatred against the Jews in the Western nations of the world. In Japan, anti-Semitic literature is being published for the first time. In the Soviet Union, a group called *Pamyat* is responsible for many anti-Semitic attacks upon Soviet Jews. In Israel, the continuing problem with the Palestinians and the PLO has been used by many groups to stir up anti-Semitic and anti-Israel feelings.

As Christians, we must remember that Israel is not a Christian nation. The leaders of Israel, like those of all nations, are both good and bad. We need not agree with everything Israel does politically or with its treatment of the Palestinians. We must, however, be very careful not to project the actions of a nation, whether good or bad, onto all individuals who ethnically or religiously are a part of that nation.

Witnessing is always individual and personal. Jewish people must be accepted and loved on the basis of their individuality and not judged as a part of a whole. Anti-Semitism and anti-Semites, in particular, always look for the worst in the Jewish people or in the nation of Israel. *If they cannot find anything, they will invent something.* They then project this "invention" upon all Jews. Believers need to be very careful not to lump all Jewish people together and judge them accordingly, or any other ethnic or religious group, for that matter.

### Dual Covenant Doctrine

Another, more subtle yet dangerous form of anti-Semitism is the *Dual Covenant* or *Two Covenant* doctrine. This teaching is becoming increasingly popular among Christians. It says that Jews do not need the Gospel because (according to this teaching) they are saved on the basis of the Abrahamic and Mosaic covenants. This doctrine holds that Gentiles, however, are under the Noaic Covenant and, as such, need to believe in Jesus.

This doctrine further contends that based on the Noaic Covenant and on the teachings of Jesus, Gentile Christians are to love the Jewish people and the nation of Israel. They are to give comfort and assistance to them, but they need not witness to Jewish people because, they say, Jews are saved through their own covenant relationship with God. Some of this teaching is the result of some Christians' reactions to the Holocaust.

Some Christians have accepted this teaching and have unwittingly replaced anti-Semitism with "Philo Israelism" (love for Israel and the Jewish people). Both extremes are dangerous. Embracing Philo Israelism without witnessing to Jewish people results in not giving them an opportunity to hear the Gospel. Without the Gospel of the Lord Jesus, Jewish people are just as lost as Gentile people. Thus, while anti-Semitism has the potential for destroying the very life and limb of the Jewish individual, Philo Israelism has the potential for allowing them to perish in a Christless eternity, thus destroying their very souls.

The words of Jesus should serve as a warning to all believers when they fail to bring the Gospel to the Jewish people or to any people, for that matter. They should serve as a warning against loving, assisting, and giving comfort without witnessing. He said, "And fear not them which kill the body, but are not able to kill the soul: but rather fear him which is able to destroy both soul and body in hell" (Matthew 10:28).

### True Believers and the Jewish People

Many people who call themselves Christians support anti-Semitism. But the question remains: Can anyone love the God of Israel and be an anti-Semite? True followers of Yeshua—those who are filled with the love of which John and Paul spoke (Galatians 6:10; 1 John 4:19-21)—answer this question with a resounding "NO!!" Thank God there have always been those who are *true believers*.

Jewish people naturally tend to associate all Christians with the hatred and ill-treatment of those who have called themselves by the Messiah's name. However, there have been many examples throughout history of real Christians—those who could, by their behavior, be recognized as belonging to the Lord; those who have shown God's love to His chosen people through their godly behavior and actions!

*Bernard of Clairvaux,* risking his own life, confronted crusaders and stopped them from putting to death an entire Jewish community. *Oliver Cromwell,* Lord Protector of England in the seventeenth century, believing the Word of God concerning His chosen people, allowed Jewish people to return to live in England after almost five hundred years of prohibition. England prospered, whereas the economy and political life of Spain and Portugal, which expelled their Jewish populations, declined.

"The Eve of Christmas" is the title of a famous poem written in the Norwegian language. Its author was *Henrik Arnold Wergeland,* the son of a Norwegian Lutheran pastor who had been a member of the constitutional assembly which proclaimed the independence of Norway in 1814.

Elias Newman wrote, "At that time Jews were not legally permitted to enter Norway. When the Norwegian government made its first loan from the Jewish banking house of Solomon Heine in Hamburg (the uncle of Heinrich Heine), the necessary conference between the Norwegian representatives and the banker could not take place until the government issued a letter of safe conduct for the Jew. Wergeland denounced this as an absurd injustice and in 1841 issued a pamphlet in which he appealed, from an ethical and humanitarian standpoint, for the removal of discriminations against Jews. He pointed out the advantages which Denmark and Sweden had derived from granting emancipation to Jews.

"Wergeland died in 1845. One of the last letters to reach him before his death was from the Danish Jewish poet Meir Aaron Goldsmidt, who wrote, 'When I think of you I am proud to be a human being.'

"The Jews of Norway and Sweden raised a monument in grateful memory of Wergeland in Oslo, Norway. And the Jews of

Fargo, N.D., placed a monument of the poet in the city park of that town.

"His collection of poetry, 'The Jew,' published in 1842 contains 'The Eve of Christmas.'. . . It tells the story of a Jewish peddler who gives his own life in vain to save from freezing to death the little daughter of a farmer couple who had refused him admission to their home on Christmas Eve. This narrative of the tragic experience of the Jewish peddler brought a valuable and humiliating lesson to the Christians and was instrumental in changing the attitude of the Norwegian people toward the Jews. Since then, Norway has shown a remarkable interest in the spiritual and material welfare of Israel and has set an outstanding example for other nations to follow.

"The promise of God to bless those that bless Israel has been fulfilled in the experience of the Nordic nation. God gave the Church of Norway the learned and pious Jewish Christian scholar, Dr. Carl Paul Caspari, who for fifty years served as theological professor at Oslo University and who, as a friend and collaborator of Gisle Johnsen, wielded a blessed influence upon the spiritual life of the Scandinavian people" (Elias Newman, *Hebrew Christian Alliance Quarterly,* n.d.).

*King Christian of Denmark* himself wore the yellow Mogen David armband forced upon Jews by the German occupation during World War II and requested that his subjects follow suit. Few Danes were seen, thereafter, without the insignia—making it impossible to distinguish Jews from non-Jews.

Many true believers risked their own lives and the lives of their families to save Jewish people from the cruel fate planned and executed by the Nazis. They believed God's promise: "I will bless them that bless thee, and curse them that curseth thee" (Genesis 12:3). Christians such as *Corrie Ten Boom* and her family loved the Jewish people because they first loved Israel's God!

We also see that God's promise to bless those who were a blessing to His people, the Jews, has been literally fulfilled in the United States. America opened her doors to Jews, allowing them freedoms and opportunities unavailable elsewhere. Jewish people have flourished here, playing an important role in this nation's progress and becoming an integral part of American life. Under President Harry S Truman, the United States made the decision to support a Jewish nation in Palestine. Israel would not exist if this stand had not been made by the United States.

This positive attitude of the United States toward the Jewish people has resulted in the special blessings that America has received at God's hand, blessings that have made it the powerful and prosperous nation it is today.

### True Believers' Responsibility

Terrible deeds have been done in the name of a loving God who sent His only Son to die in atonement for the sins of all mankind. These deeds cannot be ignored. True believers must recognize Satan's hand in anti-Semitism wherever they find it and seek to point Jewish people not to a religion, not to those who call themselves "Christians," but to Yeshua the Messiah, the Lord, who is the Author and Finisher of salvation.

Whatever has happened in the past, whatever evil deeds have been committed against the Jewish people, *you* can be a continuous and positive testimony to your Jewish friend. Showing love, deep and genuine, for the Jewish people and for Israel will not erase the years of persecution, but it will help to destroy the stereotype that Gentiles are anti-Semites, which so many Jewish people accept as true.

In addition to their personal example of right and positive attitudes and behavior as true followers of Yeshua, believers might also acquaint their Jewish friends with the involvement of Christians in organizations and endeavors aiding the state of Israel.

Many Christians do support Israel and show love for the Jewish people. Some have contributed to such causes as reforestation of Israel or the Mogen David Adom (Israeli Red Cross); some have invested in Israeli bonds. Others have utilized political involvement, encouraging the U.S. government to actively support Israel. The concern and demonstrated love of real followers of Yeshua will go far to blot out the dark deeds of the past and present a positive testimony to Jewish people—a testimony which will have considerable influence as Christians seek to share their faith in Messiah!

Believers must remember, however, that although showing love, concern, and comfort to the Jewish people is important, it is no substitute for witnessing and sharing the Gospel with them. All believers are responsible to witness and to share their faith with Jewish people. Simply loving Israel and the Jewish people without witnessing to them and sharing the Gospel with them is like the warden of a prison telling a prisoner how much he cares for him, how concerned he is for him, but never letting the prisoner know that he has received notice of a reprieve from his sentence and is, in reality, free.

Real love and true concern for the Jewish people compel believers to share the Good News of salvation that Yeshua came, died, was buried, and arose for the forgiveness of sin for Jew and Gentile alike.

## JUDAISM TODAY

The majority of Jews living in the United States and Israel are not religious. Those who are religious practice various forms of Rabbinic (not Biblical) Judaism. Remember, however, that each Jewish person is different, and since Judaism has never adopted creeds or dogmas, each Jew is free to set aside or add concepts.

### Chasidic Judaism

*Chasid* means "pious one." Chasidism is not so much a body of teachings as it is a way of life. The pattern of Chasidic life, dominated by Torah and Talmudic Law, Kabbalah, and the teachings of the Baal Shem Tov (a pious and saintly rabbi of eighteenth-century Poland), shapes and regulates the community without which it cannot exist. Chasidic Judaism stresses spontaneity and enthusiasm, but it does not oppose tradition. It emphasizes the following:

- The omnipresence of God
- Personal faith as opposed to legalism
- Superiority of experience over knowledge
- Great religious significance of Jewish women

- Prayer's efficacy when generated by selflessness and infused with emotion
- Personal loyalty to their spiritual leaders

Chasidism began as a reaction to the studious intellectualism in Orthodox Judaism. It contained a vitalizing enthusiasm which led to ecstatic worship and a feeling of brotherhood and community.

Today, Chasidic communities may be found in several of the larger cities of North America, Europe, and Israel. Recently there have been a revival and reform movement within Chasidism, but the strictness and rigidity of the Chasidic life style encourage few converts.

## Orthodox Judaism

Orthodoxy is the most highly structured form of Judaism. It is based upon the Torah as interpreted by the "Oral Law" presented by the Talmud. In fact, the Talmud is considered the final authority on all matters of faith, morality, and life in general.

### Thirteen Articles of Jewish Faith

Maimonides, one of the two greatest rabbis of the Medieval Period, expounded the chief principles of Jewish faith and then summarized them in thirteen articles. The "Thirteen Articles of Jewish Faith" are the cornerstone of Orthodox Judaism:

1. I believe with perfect faith that the Creator, blessed be his name, is the Author and Guide of everything that has been created, and that he alone has made, does make, and will make all things.
2. I believe with perfect faith that the Creator, blessed be his name, is a Unity, and that there is no unity in any manner like unto his, and that he alone is our God, who was, is, and will be.
3. I believe with perfect faith that the Creator, blessed be his name, is not a body, and that he is free from all the accidents of matter, and that he has not any form whatsoever.
4. I believe with perfect faith that the Creator, blessed be his name, is the first and the last.

5. I believe with perfect faith that to the Creator, blessed be his name, and to him alone, it is right to pray, and that it is not right to pray to any being besides him.

6. I believe with perfect faith that all the words of the prophets are true.

7. I believe with perfect faith that the prophecy of Moses our teacher, peace be unto him, was true, and that he was the chief of the prophets, both of those that preceded and of those that followed him.

8. I believe with perfect faith that the whole Law, now in our possession, is the same that was given to Moses our teacher, peace be unto him.

9. I believe with perfect faith that this law will not be changed, and that there will never be any other law from the Creator, blessed be his name.

10. I believe with perfect faith that the Creator, blessed be his name, knows every deed of the children of men, and all their thoughts, as it is said, It is he that fashioned the hearts of them all, that giveth heed to all their needs.

11. I believe with perfect faith that the Creator, blessed be his name, rewards those that keep his commandments, and punishes those that transgress them.

12. I believe with perfect faith in the coming of the Messiah, and, though he tarry, I will wait daily for his coming.

13. I believe with perfect faith that there will be a resurrection of the dead at the time when it shall please the Creator, blessed be his name, and exalted be the remembrance of him for ever and ever.

In addition to these principles, the code of obligatory duties, both positive and negative, is incumbent upon Orthodox Jews. These observances and commandments are known as *Mitzvah,* good deeds. It is by observance of the *Mitzvah* that Jewish people please God and express their love for Him.

Orthodox Judaism has declined in recent years as liberalism and agnosticism have become prevalent. Orthodox communities exist in all the larger cities. In Orthodox and Chasidic Judaism, it is imperative that kosher foods be available and that a synagogue be within walking distance because of Shabbat prohibitions. Orthodox synagogues may continue to thrive even in small communities where there is no substantial Jewish community, simply because Shabbat laws forbid extended travel.

## Conservative Judaism

Conservative Judaism is an attempt to modernize Orthodoxy; to make it more flexible and to create a form more relevant to the needs, practices, and experiences of Western society. Conservative congregations vary concerning the nature of their teachings and practices: Some are more Orthodox or more Reformed than others. Although some Conservative Jews hold to Maimonides' Thirteen Articles, others do not.

Conservative Jews are best defined by their differences from Orthodox and Reform Jews. Orthodoxy precludes any capacity for change or development. Conservative Judaism does not. Reform Judaism rejects legalism and tradition and reduces Judaism to ethical and moral creeds. Conservatives continue to follow tradition, using Hebrew in their services and adhering loosely to the system of *Kashrut* (kosher).

Conservative Judaism has attempted to make the best of both worlds. Clinging to the teachings of Biblical and Talmudic masters, it has yet enabled Jews to live inconspicuously and comfortably in the modern world.

## Reform Judaism

The Reform movement began in the nineteenth century as a response to the growing modernization and liberalization of the Western world. Traditional Judaism had become, for some, a burden impeding their progress in society, education, and business. Large numbers of German Jews began to assimilate in order to gain emancipation from the ghetto. To stem the tide of assimilation, Reform Judaism was born.

Reform Judaism is more of an ethical and religious creed than it is a way of life. Reform Jews can practice their Judaism without the need of a Jewish community or even a temple. Their life style does not differ appreciably from that of their non-Jewish neighbors. To Reform Jews, the Bible and the Talmud are good books written with much wisdom by pious men, but these books are in no way authoritative in their lives.

In 1937 the Central Conference of American Rabbis adopted an official declaration of faith known as the "Guiding Principles of Reform Judaism," which are as follows:

1. **God**—The heart of Judaism and its chief contribution to religion is the doctrine of the One, living God, who rules the world through law and love. In Him all existence has its creative source and mankind its ideal of conduct. Though transcending time and space, He is the indwelling Presence of the world. We worship Him as the Lord of the universe and as our merciful Father.
2. **Man**—Judaism affirms that man is created in the Divine image. His spirit is immortal. He is an active co-worker with God. As a child of God, he is endowed with moral freedom and is charged with the responsibility of overcoming evil and striving after ideal ends.
3. **Torah**—God reveals Himself not only in the majesty, beauty, and orderliness of nature but also in the vision and moral striving of the human spirit. Revelation is a continuous process, confined to no one age. Yet the people of Israel, through its prophets and sages, achieved unique insight in the realm of religious truth. The Torah, both written and oral, enshrines Israel's ever-growing conscious-ness of God and of the moral law. . . . Each age has the obligation to adapt the teachings of the Torah to its basic needs in consonance with the genius of Judaism.
4. **Israel**—Judaism is the soul of which Israel is the body. Living in all parts of the world, Israel has been held together by the ties of a common history, and above all, by the heritage of faith.

Clearly, Reform Judaism is more concerned with justice, peace, and ethical behavior than it is with holiness or God-consciousness. Only those who strive for moral goals are truly seeking God according to its teachings. And God, Himself, is not much more than a moral concept.

## Reconstructionism

The Reconstructionist movement, a recent adaptation of Judaism, was founded by Rabbi Mordecai M. Kaplan in the United States. Based on the premise that Judaism needed to be "reconstructed" along the lines which would provide goals and ethics for this life, Reconstructionism denies the existence of life after death and the need for eternal salvation.

Reconstructionism defines Judaism as an "evolving religious civilization." The essence of its philosophy and teaching is *neither Biblical nor Talmudic,* but revolves around the continuous, ongoing life of the Jewish people. The culture, history, language, and ideals of Judaism support Jewish life. "Religion," as such, is merely one facet of this existence.

Dr. Kaplan maintains that the synagogue, or temple, must be the center of *all* expressions of Jewish life, including religious, but not excluding social or cultural areas. Because belief in God is unnecessary to Jewish life, according to Kaplan, nonreligious Jews should be allowed involvement in the synagogal society.

Unlike other forms of Judaism, Reconstructionism has imposed itself upon the religious and nonreligious alike. Educators, social workers, and even rabbis have been impressed to reconsider standard, generally accepted ideas. "Jewish survival" has become less religion-oriented. Jewish people who have long since rejected Judaism have begun to reinvolve themselves in Jewish life apart from religion. Thus, Reconstructionism has had a momentous impact upon Jewish life in the United States, among religious as well as secular Jews—all of whom find a place within the Reconstructionist scheme of Jewish society.

## Secular Humanism

The majority of Jewish people today are not religious, but are agnostic, believing that if there is a God, it is all but impossible to know Him. Their ties with synagogues or temples are limited to events such as marriage, birth, and death. They may be involved in the local Jewish community center for social reasons: They hope that their children will meet and marry Jews. Culturally, ethnically, and socially—but not religiously—they are Jewish.

In almost every sense, these Jewish people differ little from their neighbors. Their interests, politics, education, and socioeconomic situations are not determined by the fact that they are Jewish. They are nominally involved in Judaism, as their Catholic or Protestant neighbors are nominally "Christian." They are cultural, rather than religious, Jews—basing their lives on high humanist principles rather than on the teachings of Judaism. In every way these Jewish people are secular.

Others of your Jewish friends and neighbors will be involved in the "New Age Movement" or in one of the many cults hiding under its wide umbrella. The New Age Movement disguises itself under a number of different names. It is called the Human Potential Movement, the Perennial Philosophy, or Perennial Wisdom. Its basic tenets are as follows: (1) God is not personal, but a force. (2) Because this force is in everything, there is no death. (3) You can be like God. (4) The secret is in knowledge.

Many secular Jews are involved in some aspect of the New Age Movement or in one of the cults. In a study of ex-cult members, 21 percent of the people coming out of cultic groups like Scientology or the Divine Light Mission were Jewish. It is estimated that over 12 percent of the Unification Church, founded by Sun Myung Moon, is made up of Jewish people. Such involvement on the part of Jewish people in quasi-religious cults should not come as a surprise to believers.

Jewish people have a *special, God-given spiritual hunger.* Paul says, "For I bear them record that they have a zeal of God, but not according to knowledge" (Romans 10:2). Jewish people who reject the truth of God's Word, or who have never had an opportunity to hear the Gospel, oftentimes turn to substitute messiahs—false religions and false gospels—to fill that God-given vacuum. The New Age Movement and religious cults allow Jewish people to express this "zeal for God," but with new, broad-minded definitions that anyone can embrace. In accepting these teachings, Jewish people avoid persecution and at the same time find acceptance from other groups within society.

Interestingly, the majority of these Jewish people who are secular or who are involved in New Age Movement or other cultic groups are still vitally interested in and even involved with Israel. They contribute to Zionist organizations and projects, read with concern the most recent news of the Middle East, and visit Israel as often as they are able. Their Jewishness is based more upon a commitment to the land of their fathers than to any religious creed or philosophy. To them, Israel is the essence of their Jewishness.

### Zionism

There are few Jewish people of religious or nonreligious persuasion who are not interested in the welfare of Israel and of their people who are undergoing persecution in Soviet Union or in the Arab countries. Most Jews consider themselves to be Zionists. That is, they believe in and work for the continued existence of a Jewish national homeland and state. This does *not* make them any less loyal to the country in which they reside!

Jewish people, for the most part, have a special love for the land which God gave to their fathers, Abraham, Isaac, and Jacob, and to their people for all time. God has placed within them a desire for this land which draws them irresistibly. Very few Jews are aware of the God-directed nature of their feelings for Israel, especially since they do not look upon the Bible as the inspired Word of God. But they do regard Israel as their traditional homeland, as the center of Jewish culture, and as their unforsakeable heritage.

Israel unites Jews of all religious and nonreligious inclinations in a common cause of love and concern.

# Approaching Your Jewish Friends

In approaching a Jewish person, it is imperative that you consider everything you say and do according to Jesus' command: "And as ye would that men should do to you, do ye also to them" (Luke 6:31).

## CREATING FRIENDSHIPS

Build bridges, *not* walls! So often in witnessing, in our zeal to share the wonderful life we have through Jesus, we may become overbearing and patronizing. In order to be effective witnesses, it is always necessary that we maintain a prayerful spirit, an understanding heart, and a ready ear. We must especially be truthful and patient.

Witnessing is most effectively done with friends. Friendship is the greatest extension of God's love, but it must be cultivated. It is impossible to be a friend to someone if our only concern is for his soul. Friendship involves relationships with people who are not yet where the Lord wants them to be. These relationships make us vulnerable.

Creating such a relationship is an art and requires skill. It involves laying the proper foundation, rooted in the love of God. Friendships are based on common interests such as children, sports, music, art, jogging, work, hobbies, literature, chess, and so forth. The Bible tells us that if we are desirous of having friends, we must show ourselves to be friendly (Proverbs 18:24). We, then, as believers should be establishing friendships with our neighbors and associates at work or school. Making friends and building friendships should be the responsibility of every believer.

We should especially let our Jewish friends know that we are not seeking friendships just to try and "convert" them to Christianity. Instead, we should communicate by our actions and words that friends are important because of our relationship with God and that because of this relationship, their friendship is important to us as well.

## SHARING OUR TESTIMONIES

Having established an avenue of communication with a Jewish person, we will naturally find the opportunity to describe our relationship with the Messiah Yeshua. There are a number of things to keep in mind.

### Making Our Testimonies Personal

■ We can make our testimony *personal* by describing how real and relevant God is in our life.

■ We can share how He answers specific prayers, and how He fills life with joy and peace. Remember, whatever we share must be *real*, and it must be properly motivated.

### Handed Down from the Prophets

■ The Holy Scriptures, which teach about God, were written by Jewish prophets. Everything we have been describing was given to us by God through the Jewish people.

■ Our faith is directly related to the faith of Abraham, according to the book of Hebrews.

■ Through the Jewish prophets we learn that people are cut off from God by sin and that they can be reconciled only by a blood atonement (Leviticus 17:11).

■ Jewish writers declared God's promise of the Messiah and the fulfillment of this promise as well. And Jewish believers in Yeshua, the Messiah (almost all of the early believers were Jewish), carried this Good News to the Gentiles.

■ If God loves the Jewish people, as He declares in Jeremiah 31:3, 4, then how can *we* do otherwise? Some people who call themselves "Christians" have persecuted Jewish people, but according to the New Covenant, no true follower of Yeshua can hate anyone (Galatians 6:10; 1 John 4:19-21), especially not Yeshua's own people!

■ God has promised to bless the world through the Jewish people (Genesis 12:3). Part of this promise was fulfilled in the first coming of the Messiah, but part of it is yet to be completed when He returns to reign from Jerusalem for a thousand years (*see* "Prophecy Concerning Israel").

## EMPHASIZING ISRAEL

■ All true Bible believers should know prophecy relevant to Israel—past, present, and future (*see* "Prophecy Concerning Israel")—as well as about current events. Israel is usually a common denominator among Jewish people, so your Jewish friend will be surprised and pleased at your interest in Israel. The more you know about Israel, the better! But remember, your enthusiasm must be genuine.

■ You might begin by asking your Jewish friend if he has been to Israel, what he saw, and so forth. Perhaps tell him that you too would like to visit Israel.[1] Ask questions! But remember, share your concern for Israel as it is *today*, not just as it was two thousand years ago.

■ When the time is right (you should always be in prayer about this), share your assurance of God's plan for Israel. You can also ask if he is interested in reading about God's promises to Israel, because you know that God keeps His promises.

■ As you declare your concern for the state and people of Israel, explain that true followers of Messiah believe in the Bible as God's inspired Word and that they support the nation of Israel and always will, despite Arab demands or oil shortages!

---

[1]To avoid using terms such as *he and she* and *his and her* throughout, we have used only the masculine. However, these guidelines apply to *all* Jewish people.

## SHARING THE MESSAGE OF THE MESSIAH

In order to present the Good News of Messiah's atoning death and glorious resurrection, you must first lay some ground work. In preparation for witnessing, you should cultivate certain characteristics:

■ You must love the Lord, love His living Word, and love the things He loves: He wept over Jerusalem because He loved His people so much!

■ You must pray fervently for the Jewish people and especially for your Jewish contacts.

■ You must believe and *study* the Bible: It is necessary to have knowledge before you can share it with others.

■ You must have a genuine love and concern for Jewish people: Don't ever be phony in your relationships with them.

■ You must be *patient:* Don't expect results overnight. Remember how long you were in unbelief before you accepted His gracious offer of salvation.

■ You must be sensitive to individual feelings and needs of Jewish people (*review* "Understanding Jewish People").

■ You must recognize the power and leading of the Holy Spirit: Anything done in your own strength will inevitably fail.

■ It is essential that you fully understand God's plan for mankind and Messianic prophecy before you attempt to witness to your Jewish friend (*see* "Use of Scripture").

### Creating Spiritual Interest

■ Be sure to use proper terminology (*review* "Do's and Don'ts of Terminology").

■ Wear a Jewish symbol such as a Mogen David (Star of David), a "Shalom" pin or pendant, an Israeli flag pin, and so forth. When asked, explain that you identify with the Jewish people and Israel because of the Bible.

■ Ask questions about Jewish holidays, customs, and food (remember, your interest must be genuine).

■ Visit your friend's synagogue or temple and show your interest in his religious practices.

■ Stay in close fellowship with the Lord and live such a life style before your friend so that he will be envious (Romans 11:11). Radiate the love, joy, and peace that we have talked about (Galatians 2:20). Let your relationships with family and friends speak for you.

■ Show an interest in Israel, expressing concern for the problems it faces. Be prepared to explain God's watchful care over Israel and your assurance that Israel will survive (*see* "Prophecy Concerning Israel"). Emphasize points that will attract your Jewish friend to the Messiah. Your faith is very Jewish. In fact, it is permeated with Jewishness. Convey this feeling to your friend.

■ Your friend says, "I was born a Jew and I will die a Jew." *Of course!* What could be *more Jewish* than a Jew accepting the promised Jewish Messiah? Gentiles are grafted into the Jewish olive tree according to Romans 11:17-25. Jewish people do not give up their Jewish heritage or identity; they gain a personal relationship with the God of Israel through Yeshua, the promised Jewish Messiah, and thus their identity as Jews becomes spiritual as well as physical.

■ The faith which you are sharing with your Jewish friend came from the Jewish people. The Bible is a Jewish book—both Old and New Covenants. The Savior is Jewish! The early "missionaries" to the nations (Gentiles) were Jews. Paul (Rabbi Saul), the most prominent of them, retained his Jewishness (Acts 18:18) and referred to it with great satisfaction and pride (Romans 11:1; 2 Corinthians 11:22).

■ You are *not* telling your Jewish friend about a religion, but about a personal relationship with the God of his forefathers—Abraham, Isaac, and Jacob. "Religion" is manmade, but a *relationship* with God is based on man's positive response to God's provisions for salvation and reconciliation and results in a closeness to God experienced by men like Abraham, Moses, and David.

■ Other Jewish people, including rabbis and intellectuals, have come to believe that Yeshua is the promised Jewish Messiah through their study of the Bible.

■ Challenge your Jewish friend to read Messianic Scriptures from his own Bible (*see* "Messianic Prophecy and Typology") and discuss the Scriptures with him. Ask him to pray that God will show him if Yeshua is the Messiah (don't expect him to accept Yeshua immediately—be patient and willing to wait for further opportunities to discuss the Scriptures with him).

■ If your Jewish friend is involved in the New Age Movement or in other occult or cultic practices, stress also the *authority of the Scriptures.* Point out that a Jewish person cannot define his existence apart from the Word of God. Further, emphasize that in the Scriptures the nation of Israel was warned by God that if its people participated in occult practices, the land would be given to other nations. Share how Israel's involvement in idolatry; the occult; and false religious practices—those that are apart from belief in the God of Abraham, Isaac, and Jacob—resulted in judgment on the nation and its people.

Point out that the truth of Scripture remains objective and that we ourselves do not possess the ultimate source of truth apart from the Word of God. One writer expressed it this way: "You can think water, you can meditate water, but if you don't drink water eventually you will die. So it is with the water of life—with the truth of God's Word. Without accepting it we will die."

## FOLLOWING UP

At this point you may want to read—and then recommend to your Jewish friends who have accepted Yeshua—the Chosen People Ministries' book entitled, *How to Be Like the Messiah: Walking the New Halakhah,* by John Bell. This book has been especially prepared and written for new Jewish believers. It is the companion volume to this witnessing book. It expands on many of the areas of discipleship which are discussed in this book. Copies of *How to Be Like the Messiah* can be ordered by writing to Chosen People Ministries, Inc. (see the Order Form).

When your Jewish friend does come to a saving knowledge of the Messiah, do not feel that you should revert to traditional "Christian" language, and so forth. Continue to be sensitive to his special difficulties involving Jewish family and friends. Do not suggest negative actions (such as disassociating himself from his synagogue or temple, and so forth).

Here are a few positive suggestions:

- Tell your Jewish friend to pray about all decisions.
- Carefully discuss the plan of salvation and pray with him.
- Plan a time when you can study the Bible together (on a weekly basis, if possible). Share principles of the faith that will help him grow spiritually, such as the power of prayer, daily prayer and Bible reading, assurance of salvation, the fruits of the Spirit, and guides for studying the Bible. If your Jewish friend does not have a New Covenant, suggest that he get one or give him one.
- Invite him to go with you to a Bible-centered and doctrinally sound Messianic congregation if there is one in your area. Be sure that you have attended the congregation before you invite your friend, so you will know firsthand what the congregation teaches, how they conduct their services, and so forth. If you are uncertain about the Messianic congregations in your area, you may wish to contact Chosen People Ministries, Inc. We have listings of Messianic congregations, and we can let you know if there is one in your area.
- Invite him to a small home Bible study, preferably one in which other Jewish believers are involved (remember, Gentile-style worship and churches may still frighten him).
- Introduce your Jewish friend to other believers who will encourage him spiritually and with whom he will feel comfortable.
- Help your Jewish friend see that the best way to share his faith with family members and friends is to demonstrate it. Believing in Jesus as the Messiah should make him a better Jew, not divide him from the Jewish people. Share the lessons you learned in "Do's and Don'ts of Terminology," "Approaching Your Jewish Friends," and "Messianic Prophecy and Typology."
- Explain that life will not be perfect but that God promises to be close to him and to help him no matter what problems he faces.
- Tell him *how* God answers prayer—that God will always do what is best and that we should always pray that God's will be done in our lives.

■ Help him realize that believers must keep their eyes on the Lord (we are fallible, but He is not) and must allow the Holy Spirit to guide us through prayer and through the Word.

■ Above all, continue your friendship and let your Jewish friend know that he can always come to you with his problems. You may not be able to answer all his questions or solve all his problems, but you can pray with him and continue to show God's love, especially now that you share a faith in the God of Israel through Yeshua, the Messiah.

If you have any questions about Jewish culture, religious practices, the pronunciation of Hebrew or Yiddish words, and so forth, feel free to ask your Jewish friend, the local rabbi, Hebrew teacher, or any other religious leader. Any of these people will be happy to answer any question motivated by sincere interest. And you will have the opportunity to make another friend or deepen an existing friendship through your common interest.

# Use of Scripture

Your understanding of the Tenach (Old Covenant) is essential to an effective witness. It is important that you understand God's plan of redemption for mankind, prophecies concerning the Messiah, and prophetic truths about Israel.

The use of a Jewish Bible (one published by a Jewish publisher for Jews) may be imperative since most Jewish people think that their Bible is different from the "Gentile Bible" (they may even be surprised at your knowledge of the Tenach). You can use any translation which includes the New Covenant, such as the King James Version, New International Version, New American Standard Version, and so forth. Weave your use of Scripture into the approach that has already been discussed. Be natural; don't force it on your friend.

## UNDERSTANDING GOD'S PLAN AND MAN'S NEEDS

1. God loves man and desires that all men should experience a life filled with His blessings.
   - *Deuteronomy 6:3*—God promised blessings to the Israelites if they would obey Him.
   - *Psalm 16:11*—There is fullness of joy with the Lord, and His way is the path of life.
   - *Psalm 36:7-10*—The lovingkindness of the Lord is excellent.
   - *Isaiah 41:10*—The Lord provides peace, courage, strength, and endurance in the face of life's problems.

2. Man is separated from God by sin: He is a sinner by nature and by will.
   - *Job 15:14-16*—Man is totally unclean in God's sight.
   - *Psalm 53:2-4*—There is *no one* who is righteous but God.
   - *Psalm 130:3, 4*—We cannot stand before the Lord if our iniquities are counted against us.
   - *Psalm 143:2*—In God's eyes, no man can justify himself.
   - *Ecclesiastes 7:20*—There is no man who is righteous and without sin.
   - *Isaiah 64:6*—All of our goodness is as filthy rags to God.
   - *Jeremiah 17:9*—The human heart is deceitful and wicked.

3. The result of sin and separation from God is spiritual death.
   - *Isaiah 59:2, 3*—God cannot have fellowship with sinners.
   - *Jeremiah 31:30*—Every man shall die for his sins.
   - *Ezekiel 18:4*—The soul guilty of sin will die.

4. Man is unable to find reconciliation with God through his own efforts or good deeds.
   - *Job 14:4*—No one can make something clean out of something unclean.
   - *Psalm 49:7*—No man can redeem another man.
   - *Proverbs 20:9*—No one can say they are free from sin.
   - *Jeremiah 2:22*—Nothing man can do will wash away his sin.

5. God has provided a way by which reconciliation can be accomplished. Atonement is available through the Messiah as a free gift to all men.
   - *Leviticus 17:11*—Only a blood sacrifice atones for sin.
   - *Psalm 49:15*—God promises to redeem the soul from death's power.
   - *Isaiah 43:11, 25*—Only the Lord can provide salvation and forgive sins.
   - *Isaiah 53:3-12*—Messiah suffered and died bearing the sins of humanity that those who trust in Him might be justified.

6. The Messiah's atoning death may be appropriated unto salvation by faith in its efficacy.
   - *Genesis 15:6*—Abraham, the father of the Jewish people, was counted righteous because of his faith (not because of his good deeds).
   - *Nahum 1:7*—The Lord knows those who trust in Him and provides security for them.
   - *Habakkuk 2:4*—The righteous man lives by his faith.
7. Only by repentance of sin and acceptance of Yeshua the Messiah as Savior, through prayer by faith, can reconciliation be made with God.
   - *Psalm 32:1-5*—Forgiveness and justification are brought about by confession of sin.
   - *Proverbs 28:13*—God will be merciful to those who confess and forsake their sins.

## MESSIANIC PROPHECY AND TYPOLOGY

The disciples, apostles, and all the early followers of Jesus believed in and preached about Him *without* the New Covenant; it had not yet been written. They used Old Covenant Scriptures to identify Him, to explain His dual ministry (as the sacrificial Lamb and as the coming King), and to demonstrate man's need of His atonement. Jesus Himself said, "Had ye believed Moses [and the other prophets], ye would have believed me: for he wrote of me" (John 5:46).

Those who *did* believe the words of the prophets *concerning the Messiah* accepted Him, knowing (and as He declared) that "all things must be fulfilled, which were written in the Law of Moses, and in the Prophets, and in the Psalms" (Luke 24:44).

### Messianic Prophecies Fulfilled by Jesus

The following verses from the New Covenant (at right) illustrate how Jesus fulfilled the Old Covenant Messianic prophecies (at left).

I. *Who Was the Messiah to Be?*
   - He was to be of a woman's seed.

   Genesis 3:15                  Galatians 4:4

- He would be descended from Abraham.
  Genesis 22:18      Galatians 3:16
- He would be from the line of David.
  2 Samuel 7:8-16      Luke 3:23-28
  Isaiah 11:1      Matthew 1
  Jeremiah 23:5, 6      Acts 13:22, 23
       Romans 15:12
- He was to be of the tribe of Judah.
  Genesis 49:10      Hebrews 7:14
       Revelation 5:5
- He would be born of a virgin as a special *sign* to the world.
  Isaiah 7:14      Matthew 1:23
- He would be born at a specific time.
  Genesis 49:10      Galatians 4:4
  Daniel 9:24, 25
- He was to be born in Bethlehem.
  Micah 5:2      Matthew 2:1
- He would be preceded by a forerunner.
  Malachi 3:1      Matthew 3:1-12
  Isaiah 40:3      Luke 1:17

II. *Aspects of His Ministry*
- He was to be a prophet like Moses.
  Deuteronomy 18:18, 19      Acts 3:20-23
- He would be specially anointed by the Spirit of God.
  Isaiah 11:2; 61:1, 2      Matthew 3:16, 17
       Luke 4:16-21
- He was to be a priest according to the order of Melchizedek (Genesis 14:18-20).
  Psalm 110:4      Hebrews 5:5, 6
- He was to be the redeemer of the Gentiles as well as the Jews.
  Genesis 49:10      Matthew 12:18-21
  Isaiah 42:1-7
- He would be God's Son.
  Psalm 2:7      Matthew 16:16; 17:5
  Proverbs 30:4      Hebrews 1:5

- He would enter Jerusalem in a specific manner.
  Zechariah 9:9          Matthew 21:1-11
- He would come suddenly upon the defilers of the Temple.
  Malachi 3:1-3          Matthew 21:12-16
- He would possess an unusual zeal for the Lord.
  Psalm 69:9             John 2:17
- Much of His teaching was to be done in parables.
  Psalm 78:2             Matthew 13:34, 35
- He would perform many miracles.
  Isaiah 35:3-6          Matthew 11:4-6
                         John 11:47, 48
- He would be a stumbling stone to His people.
  Isaiah 8:14, 15; 28:16      Romans 9:31-33
                         1 Peter 2:6-8
- His brethren would reject Him.[1]
  Psalm 69:8             John 1:11; 7:5
  Isaiah 53:3

III. *Events of His Death*
- He would be betrayed by a friend.
  Psalm 41:9             John 13:18-21
                         Acts 1:16
- He was to be "sold out" for thirty pieces of silver.
  Zechariah 11:12        Matthew 26:14, 15
- The price of His betrayal would be given to buy a "potter's field" (burial place for the poor).
  Zechariah 11:13        Matthew 27:3-10
- He would be mocked, spat upon, and beaten.
  Psalm 22:7, 8          Matthew 27:30, 31, 39-44
  Micah 5:1, 2
  Isaiah 50:6
- The details of His crucifixion were announced.[2]
  Psalm 22               Luke 22–23

---

[1] If the Jewish people *as a nation* had recognized Jesus as their Messiah, He would not have fulfilled these prophecies, would not have died, and thus, could not have been the Messiah.
[2] Crucifixion was *not* a form of Jewish execution but was invented by the Romans centuries after this prophecy was written.

- His hands and feet would be pierced.
  Psalm 22:16        John 19:18, 34, 37; 20:25-29
  Zechariah 12:10
- Not one of His bones was to be broken.
  Exodus 12:46        John 19:33-37
  Psalm 34:20
- He was to suffer thirst and be given vinegar to drink.
  Psalm 22:15; 69:21        Matthew 27:34
         John 19:28
- He would be buried among the wealthy.
  Isaiah 53:9        Matthew 27:57-60

## IV. *Purpose of His Death*

- He would make an end of sin and provide reconciliation with God.
  Daniel 9:24        Romans 3:23-26; 8:32
- He would bear the sins of the world and make intercession for transgressors.
  Isaiah 53        2 Corinthians 5:21
         Hebrews 9–10

## V. *His Resurrection and Ascension*

- His body would not even begin to decompose.
  Psalm 16:10        Acts 2:31
  Proverbs 30:4
- He would be raised from the dead.
  Psalm 2; 16:10        Acts 13:33-37
  Proverbs 30:4
- He would ascend to the chief place of honor with God to make intercession for us.
  Psalm 68:18; 110:1        Luke 24:51
         Acts 1:9
         Romans 8:34
         Hebrews 1:3

## VI. *His Future Glory*

- He shall be King and reign from David's citadel, Zion, over a spiritually revived Israel. He will be King *forever*, King of kings and Lord of lords.

Psalm 2:6; 10:16; 24:7; 110   Matthew 31:46
Isaiah 9:6, 7   1 Timothy 6:15
Zechariah 8:20-23   Revelation 17:14; 21:2-27
Daniel 2:44

### Old Covenant Messianic Types Fulfilled by Jesus

We can also understand the Messiah's role in His first coming through the sacrificial system which God gave to Israel. The necessity of a blood atonement was declared in Leviticus 17:11. Also, God clearly showed through His commandments concerning the sacrificial offerings (Leviticus 1–9) that substitutionary death was essential to redemption. Since it is no longer possible for Israel and the Jewish people to continue the sacrifices—the Temple, the only legitimate cite for sacrifices, was destroyed in A.D. 70—God must have provided another sacrifice (Hebrews 9 says, "A better sacrifice").

The Jewish holy days also clearly demonstrate the need for a substitutionary sacrifice. Yom Kippur (the Day of Atonement) was observed by the sacrifice of an animal and was made for the sins of all Israel (Leviticus 16).

Pesach (Passover) was instituted by God to remind the Jewish people (for all time) that a lamb had died so that they might live (Exodus 12; Deuteronomy 16). In fact, as the Passover has been, and still is, traditionally celebrated, the Seder involves several elements that point specifically to the Messiah:

- Elijah is invited to come in and announce the coming of the Messiah (John the Baptizer was a type of Elijah [Isaiah 40:3; Malachi 3:1; Matthew 3:1-12; Luke 1:17]).
- During the Seder, a matzah is broken into three parts. The third part, called the *Afikomen* (a Greek word meaning "I came"), is hidden to be found at the end of the service. This ceremony is believed to have

been instituted by early Jewish believers. Nonbelieving Jews have no satisfactory explanation for it.

Jesus claimed to fulfill all the prophecies concerning the Messiah's first coming. He was *not* merely a holy man or a great teacher, as some people like to suggest. *If He was not who He claimed to be, He was either self-deceived and irrational, or a complete liar!* Jesus declared that He was the Son of God, that He was equal to and one with God, and that *He was the One spoken of by the prophets.* His claim is supported by the eyewitnesses of the New Covenant who were martyred for their faith. But it is also supported by the radically changed lives of those who have believed in and have followed Him down through the centuries.

## PROPHECY CONCERNING ISRAEL

The survival of the Jewish people is the greatest miracle of history. It was predicted by the prophets of Israel centuries before the Dispersion. All the facts of Jewish survival were delineated in Scripture.

1. God made specific, unconditional promises to Abraham.
   - He promised to make of Abraham's descendants a great nation (Genesis 12:2).
   - This nation was to be blessed and to be a blessing to the world (Genesis 12:2, 3).
   - God established this covenant with Abraham (Genesis 17:7) and confirmed it with Isaac (Genesis 17:19, 21) and with Jacob (Genesis 25:23; 35:9-15).
   - It was guaranteed by God to be an eternal covenant (Genesis 17:7).
   - A specific area of land was to be given to this nation as its homeland forever (Genesis 17:8).

2. The descendants of Abraham (his grandson and greatgrandson) emigrated to Egypt during a great famine. They left Canaan as a small tribe, but returned to it as a great nation.

- Through separation and (eventually) servitude, the Jewish people retained their distinctiveness (Genesis 46).
- God promised to be with His people while they were in Egypt and to bring them out of Egypt (Genesis 46:3, 4).
- Moses was used by God to lead his people (now a nation of about two million) from Egypt (Exodus 12:37).
- God established a conditional covenant with the nation of Israel—the Mosaic Covenant (Exodus 19): The people of Israel were to keep God's Law (enabling them to be a holy nation unto God) and, in turn, God would bless them (in direct proportion to their obedience to His commandments) (Exodus 20:1-26).
- God gave the land of Canaan to Israel as He promised Abraham (Joshua 1–24).

3. Israel's ancient history is recorded in the Bible. But God's promises to Israel extend to the end of ages, to eternity.
- God's prophetic warnings echo through the Tenach: Disobedience must be punished (Leviticus 26:14-39; Deuteronomy 28:15-68).
- The prophets preached that the people repent from this disobedient spirit and warned them of the judgment which was coming (Amos 2:4).
- God's judgments on Israel for its disobedience were specified by the Bible:
  —Israel to experience continuous sorrow and distress (Leviticus 26:16); drought, famine, and desolation (Leviticus 26:20, 27-31); disease and pestilence (Leviticus 26:21-26)
  —Israel's enemies to be victorious (Leviticus 26:17)
  —Israel to be dispersed throughout the world (Deuteronomy 28:64a)
  —Jews to be persecuted and killed wherever they went (Leviticus 26:38; Deuteronomy 28:65-67)
- All of these things have happened! The miracle is that the Jewish people have been preserved *despite* all of these judgments. God's promise to Abraham also declared, "I will curse him that curseth thee. . . ." (Genesis 12:3): The peoples who

have shown animosity toward the Jews have not prospered; those who have blessed them have prospered.

- God's unconditional covenant with Abraham has remained in effect despite the disobedience and dispersion of Israel (Leviticus 26:44, 45).
- God's love and mercy toward Israel are shown in His promise to regather the Jewish people and to bring them back to their own land (Isaiah 11:11, 12; Ezekiel 36:12) and to help them rebuild the waste cities (Amos 9:14).

4. The people of Israel will always be preserved by God from annihilation, despite the horrible conditions which the Bible says will dominate the world during the time called the "Great Tribulation."

- At that time, the Jewish people will again call upon God for help and He will hear them (Zechariah 13:8, 9).
- A day will come when all nations will come against Israel—a period called the "Time of Jacob's Trouble"—and they will desire to destroy the nation, but God will save it (Zechariah 12:7-9; 14:12).
- In that day, the people of Israel will recognize the identity of Him who has fought for them, the Anointed One, Yeshua. Then they will mourn (Zechariah 12:10-14).
- The Messiah will inaugurate the New Covenant with Israel, cleansing the Jewish people from sin and reconciling them *as a nation,* with the God of their fathers (Zechariah 13:1).

## THE NEW COVENANT

The nature of the New Covenant is described in Jeremiah 31.

- A new covenant can only be made when another covenant has preceded it. God has made covenants only with Israel; thus, the New Covenant *must* be a covenant with Israel.
- According to Jeremiah 31:31-34, this new covenant, the Messianic Covenant, will be made with the nation of Israel in order to reconcile Israel to God.

■ Israel as a nation will accept the Messiah, Yeshua. He will be its King as well as its Redeemer. In that day, the eternal law of God will be written, not on tablets of stone, but on the hearts of the people. He will be their God, and they will be His people, renewing the relationship which He established with them for all time and eternity.

## AN EXPLANATION OF JEWISH OBJECTIONS

Jewish people often object to statements made by believers on sociological and historical as well as religious grounds. Many of these disagreements stem from the same difficulties which Gentiles have, but others are peculiarly Jewish. The solutions to these problems are often complex but unquestionably important. However, if your Jewish friend asks you a question to which you do not have an answer, be honest: Tell him that you will try to find it for him. Remember that arguments are futile. Always be kind and tactful.

*Objection 1:* "If there is a God, why is there so much suffering in the world? Why did He allow six million Jews to die? Why doesn't He correct all the world's problems?"

Suffering is caused by men, not by God. Man's inhumanity to his fellowman results in the atrocities we read and hear of each day. God does not motivate or approve of man's evil actions; He decries man's wickedness.

God has given man freedom of choice and will. Man is able to decide for peace or war, love or hate, but God will not interfere with man's right to make these decisions. If He did, man would just be a puppet.

Man has taken God's wonderful gift of choice and distorted and warped it. Collectively, men have decided to live apart from righteousness. They not only choose to do evil, but also to do nothing about the evil decisions of others.

But God will, in His own time, judge man for his irresponsibility and wickedness (Psalm 37:7-11; Daniel 12:2). Only those who have chosen righteously (according to God's plan) will avoid punishment.

*Objection 2:* "Religions are all alike. All of them have good points and help people to live worthwhile lives."

Religions are man-made; they are *man's way* to obtain God's approval. But faith in Yeshua is *not* a religion; it is *God's way* for mankind to be reconciled to Him. Most religions have some good aspects, but this does not mean that God is satisfied with them.

Faith in the Messiah is not *another* religion, but the fulfillment of God's promises to Israel. It is a personal relationship with the God who revealed Himself in the Holy Scriptures and the *only way* that God says individuals *can* have a personal relationship with Him.

*Objection 3:* "Jews who believe in Jesus are no longer Jews."

According to the Bible, a Jew is a descendant of Abraham, Isaac, and Jacob. One is either Gentile or Jewish by birth, and nothing can change that. When a Jewish person accepts the promised Jewish Messiah, he becomes a fulfilled Jew, in continuity with Moses and the prophets. He is a completed Jew because he is not only Jewish physically but spiritually as well.

Gentiles who accept Jesus are spiritually grafted into the Jewish olive tree of faith (Romans 11). They are then able to inherit the spiritual benefits of the Good News, along with Jews. They become children of Abraham by faith (Galatians 3:7, 29).

Jesus Himself was Jewish, as were all of His disciples and apostles. These Jews never renounced their Jewish heritage and were not considered by others to have done so. They declared their Jewishness with pride (Romans 11:1; 2 Corinthians 11:22). Jews who come to believe in Jesus today are no different.

*Objection 4:* "If Jesus is the Jewish Messiah, why don't all Jews believe in Him?"

The majority is seldom correct. Philosopher John Stuart Mill declared that if he found himself on the side of the majority in any matter, he would immediately reassess his position. The majority scoffed at the idea of a world that was round. They laughed at the advanced concepts of men like Louis Pasteur. At one time, only a small minority believed that airplanes would really fly!

Many rabbis and other Jewish leaders have accepted Jesus as the Messiah:

■ By the end of the first century, the Jewish historian Neander reported that over a million Jewish people in Israel believed Yeshua to be the Messiah.

■ In the early twentieth century, Rabbi Isaac Lichtenstein of Hungary publicly accepted Yeshua as his Messiah and his congregation followed suit.

■ Dr. Max Wertheimer, a graduate of Hebrew Union College and rabbi of a Reform congregation in Dayton, Ohio, came to believe in Yeshua.

There have always been Jews who believe in Yeshua as Messiah, and their number is steadily increasing.

Some Jewish people have rejected Yeshua because they have failed to understand His dual role. They have looked for a King, for a political leader who would free them from their oppressors and provide peace and prosperity. All this Yeshua will accomplish in the future, when He returns to reestablish the throne of David (Psalm 2:6; 110; Isaiah 9:6, 7; Zechariah 8:20-23).

The Messiah's first coming is misunderstood, although it is described in detail by the prophet Isaiah and others. The Jewish people, as a nation, did not realize that a perfect atonement could only be made by a perfect Being, God's Son, the Anointed One. Yeshua came first to die in atonement for sin, in order that men, Jews and Gentiles alike, might be reconciled to God (Isaiah 53).

*Objection 5:* "Jews don't believe in 'original sin' because their Bible doesn't teach this concept."

According to the Tenach, all men are sinful, both by nature (Genesis 5:3; 6:15) and by will (Isaiah 53:6). In Psalm 53:2-4 we read that no one is righteous. The prophet Isaiah declared that all the goodness of man is as "filthy rags" to God (Isaiah 64:6). We are told in Psalm 143:2 that *no man* can justify himself before God. Leviticus 17:11 makes it clear that only a blood sacrifice can solve the problem of sin.

It is true the many Jewish people do not believe in the concept of sin (especially secular, Reconstructionist, Reform, and some Conservative Jews). They do not believe in it because they are either ignorant of the teachings of the Tenach, or because they do not accept its teachings. Sin is not a "Christian" concept; it comes directly from the Jewish Bible.

*Objection 6:* "There are many doctrines that are unacceptable to the rabbis and are not taught in the Jewish Scriptures":

■ **The Trinity:** Believers in the Messiah do not believe in "three gods" (Galatians 3:20; 1 Timothy 2:5). Their understanding of God is from the Old Covenant as well as the New Covenant. God's nature is an incomprehensible mystery. What we do know of Him comes from His own revelation of Himself.

The plurality of God's nature is revealed in His Name, "Elohim." *Elohim* is a plural word. Genesis 1:26 and 11:6 use plural pronouns to describe God (see also Isaiah 48:16).

In the Shema, we are reminded of God's oneness (Deuteronomy 6:4), ". . . the Lord is one." The Hebrew word for "one" is *echad,* and it clearly indicates compound unity. The word *yechad,* meaning "absolute singularity," might have been used but it was not because it would have been inaccurate. In fact, *echad* is always used to describe the oneness of God; *yechad* is never used for this purpose.

■ **The Divinity:** Because most Jewish people do not understand God's true nature as revealed in the Tenach, they fail to realize that God does have a Son. Proverbs 30:4 asks the question, "What is His Son's name?" Psalm 2:7, 12 describes the need for men to submit to God's Son.

The Tenach also teaches that the Messiah would be both God and man (if God is truly all-powerful, He could certainly do this). In Isaiah 9:6, 7, He is identified as the Son of David, but at the same time the titles which belong to Him can only be given to God Himself. Isaiah 7:14 calls the Messiah "God with us" (Immanuel). According to Jeremiah 23:5, 6a, the descendant of David who will reign in complete peace is given the name which belongs only to God,

"Adonai Tzidkenu," the Lord our righteousness. David himself, in Psalm 110:1, is described as hearing a conversation addressed by the Eternal God to David's Lord—God's Son, the Messiah.

Only a perfect being could provide the proper atonement. The only perfect being is God. If God can do all things, He could surely send His Son to earth, to be born as a man, to die and be resurrected!

■ **The Virgin Birth:** With God all things are possible. Sarah conceived Isaac when she was physically past child-bearing age. Isaac was a miracle, proving God's mighty power to Abraham and Sarah (Genesis 18:11).

According to the prophet Isaiah, the Messiah's birth would be miraculous and would be a sign that He was sent by God. Isaiah 7:14 declared that a virgin would conceive. If a young woman *who was not a virgin* conceived, how would this be considered a miraculous sign?

■ **The Blood Atonement:** We know from Leviticus 17:11 and Exodus 12:13 that only a blood atonement would provide the proper covering for sin and reconcile man with God. The Messiah was promised for this reason as well as to establish His Kingdom (which He will do in the future according to Isaiah 9:6, 7; 11:1-5).

In His first coming, He was to die for the sins of Israel and the nations. He was to be the suffering Lamb of God who would take away the sins of the world. Yeshua's substitutionary sacrifice fulfilled the words of the prophets (Isaiah 53:4-6, 8, 10-12).

These issues are extremely pertinent to the question of Jewish people accepting Yeshua as the Messiah. Wait until these questions and objections arise and be prepared with answers from the Tenach. Do not present these issues yourself. If your friend is interested and the Holy Spirit is dealing with him, they will arise naturally. All that you must do is to be available.

# Use of Materials

There is a myriad of materials available for each stage in your relationship with your Jewish friend. But it is essential that you know *when* to use *what.* It is also important to understand *how* to use these materials. Be creative and innovative in your witnessing. Always be prayerful and allow the Holy Spirit to guide you. Above all, be sensitive and sensible.

During the period when you are establishing your friendship, it is best to avoid most tracts and pamphlets. A Jewish symbol worn or displayed in your home or office will interest Jewish people in you and your faith. Then you will have an opportunity to share your testimony with them (*see* "Approaching Your Jewish Friends").

Music by Jewish believers might also be used. (There are several types available at most Christian book stores, or you may order directly from Chosen People Ministries.) Ask your Jewish friend to listen with you to music cassettes produced by musicians who are Jewish believers, or present such cassettes or videos as a gift. This type of music will offer several avenues of future contact and discussion.

Chosen People Ministries has also produced a number of video cassettes which are excellent witnessing tools. These 30-minute videos are designed to present the Messiah, to provoke discussion, and to serve as a means of introducing Jewish people to their Messiah.

Another excellent witnessing tool is the Jewish calendar available through Chosen People Ministries. This is a preevangelism tool. It serves as a monthly witness to the Scriptures and to the Messiah, while providing the regular Jewish calendar with the times for the lighting of candles, Scripture readings, and so forth. This calendar, with its unique Biblical witness, is a wonderful Jewish New Year gift. Jewish calendars are always made available through Chosen People Ministries by the month of August, so that they are ready for the Jewish New Year, which begins in September/October.

When the Lord opens the door for you to offer your Jewish friend a tract or pamphlet, several questions should be considered:

- Have you read this particular piece of literature carefully?
- Is it the best tract or book for this particular person, time, place, and so forth?
- Does it relate to the specific needs and interests of your friend *now*?
- Is it an afterthought on your part, or does it "fit in" with your relationship and conversation?

If these questions can be answered affirmatively, follow these simple rules:

- Underline or highlight words or sections that seem particularly pertinent (your friend will feel more positive about reading it if he knows that you are interested in what it says).
- Loan the tract or book rather than give it to your friend. Later you can ask him for his opinion about it. This leads to discussion and involvement.
- If you have been discussing issues such as the Trinity, the virgin birth, and so forth, a pamphlet on the subject should be well received. Tracts on Jewish topics such as Yom Kippur or Passover may be presented during the appropriate season.
- Materials relevant to Israel might be introduced on Israeli Independence Day (May 12) or by some news item about Israel.

Always keep materials *relevant,* and use them *sparingly.* Chosen People Ministries has a large and varied publications/media ministry—send for catalog.

# Glossary of Jewish Terms

Many of these words are in Hebrew and Yiddish and are often used by Jewish people. (Yiddish is a combination of Hebrew, German, and some Russian and Polish, and is spoken by many European and American Jews.) Understanding these terms will help in your contacts with Jewish people.

**Greetings and Good Wishes**

*Chag Samayach* — "Happy holiday" (especially Hanukkah)

*Gut Yom Tov* — "Good holiday"

*L'Chayim* — "To life" or "To health" (a toast or salute)

*L'Hit Ra'ote* — "Until we meet again"

*L'Shanah Tovah* — "To a good year" (New Year's greeting)

*Mazel Tov* — "Good luck" or "Congratulations"

*Shalom* — "Peace" (used as "hello" or "goodbye")

*Shalom Alechem* — "Peace be unto you"

*Alechem Shalom* — "Unto you be peace" (a response to the above)

## Jewish Holy Days

*Rosh Hashanah* — New Year (celebrated in September or October) (Leviticus 23:24, 25)

*Yom Kippur* — Day of Atonement (observed with fasting and prayer for forgiveness) (Leviticus 23:26-32)

*Kol Nidre* — Means "all vows"; chanted on the eve of Yom Kippur)

*Sukkot* — Feast of Tabernacles (celebrated in "booths") (Leviticus 23:33-36)

*Sukkah* — Booth used during Sukkot for meals and/or sleeping, and so forth

*Simchat Torah* — Rejoicing Over the Law (marks the conclusion of the public, synagogal reading of the Torah each year).

*Hanukkah* — Festival of Lights (celebrates the rededication of the Temple of the Lord by the Macabees in 167 B.C.E.)

*Purim* — Feast of Esther (celebrates the victory over Haman and all who sought Jewish extinction) (Esther 9:20-32)

*Pesach* — Passover (Feast of Unleavened Bread) (Exodus 12:14-20)

*Seder* — Passover service and dinner (usually conducted on the first and second nights of Pesach)

*Haggadah* — Ritual for the Pesach service (in Hebrew and English usually)

*Matzah* — Unleavened bread

*Shabbat* — The Sabbath (Friday sunset to Saturday sunset) (Leviticus 23:3)

*Shavuot* — Means "seven weeks"; from Pesach; Feast of First Fruits (Leviticus 23:15-21); Hebrew name for Day of Pentecost mentioned in New Testament

*Bar Mitzvah* — Son of the commandment (a boy who has reached the age of religious maturity, age 13, culminating in a special ceremony)

*Barucha* — Means "blessings"; prayer offered on any occasion which calls for praise

*Bat Mitzvah* — Daughter of the commandment (a girl who has reached the age of religious maturity, 12 or 13, culminating in a special ceremony)

*Bris* — Covenant of circumcision (Genesis 17:9-14)

*Cabalah* — *Kabbalah* in Hebrew; means "transmitted teachings" or "tradition"; mystical Judaism based on *The Zohar* (*see* "Additional Reading"); concerned with Jewish speculation on the mysteries of God and the universe; derives neither from revelation nor from science, but from individual mystical speculations which became more and more esoteric; only the initiated considered capable of comprehending or communicating knowledge accumulated in this manner

*Chazzan* — Cantor (usually the leader of the service)

*Haftorah* — Section of the Prophets read immediately after the reading of the Torah in the services on Shabbat and on most holidays

*Halakhah* — Tradition, practice, rule, in Judaism

*Hallel* — Psalms of praise (root word of *hallelujah*)

*Huppah* — Bridal canopy denoting God's presence in the new home, and a reminder of the Temple at Jerusalem; symbolic of God's dwelling place with man

*Kabbalah* — Jewish mysticism; *see also* Cabalah

*Kaddish* — Means "holy"; praise to God recited in memorial to the departed

*Kashrut* — Means "kosher"; clean, acceptable food in accordance with Jewish Law (especially excluding pork and shell fish) (Deuteronomy 14:3-21)

*Ketubah* — Jewish marriage contract

*Ketuvim* — The Writings (including history and poetry)

*Kiddush* — Benediction over the "fruit of the vine" (wine) in the ceremony of sanctification of Shabbat and holidays

*Megillot* — Means "scrolls"; part of the Ketuvim, including the books of Esther (known as the *Megillah*), Lamentations, Song of Solomon, Ruth, and Ecclesiastes

*Menorah* — Candle holder; a seven-branch menorah is used (Exodus 25:31-37) except during Hanukkah, when a nine-branch menorah is used to remind Jews that a container of oil found when the Temple was being cleansed and rededicated burned for eight days instead of one day—long enough for more oil to be consecrated according to Scripture

*Mezuzah* — Parchment scroll usually in a metal container attached to the door post on the right side of the entrance to a house or room (Deuteronomy 6:9), containing the *Shema* (Deuteronomy

6:4-11) and the *Vehoyo Shamon*, section dealing with God's love and precepts (Deuteronomy 11:13-21); also worn as jewelry

*Mikvah* — Means "immerse"; ritual bath of purification

*Minyan* — Quorum needed for a service (ten men, 13 years or older)

*Mitzvah* — Command; commonly used to mean "a good deed"

*Ner Tamid* — Perpetual light signifying God's presence

*Nevi'im* — The Prophets (books of prophecy)

*Ruach Ha Codesh* — The Holy Spirit

*Shulchan Aruch* — Codified laws of Rabbinic Judaism

*Shammash* — Caretaker or sexton of the synagogue or temple

*Shema* — Jewish affirmation of faith (Deuteronomy 6:4), recited morning and evening by religious Jews and during all worship services

*Shivah* — Seven-day mourning period interrupted only on the Sabbath or major holidays

*Shule* — Another word for an Orthodox of Chasidic synagogue, from the German word for *school*; it indicates that the chief purpose of the synagogue is for the study of the Law (the Torah)

*Siddur* — Prayer book (contains prayers, Scripture, order of services)

*Synagogue* — Means "assembly"; this word usually indicates either Orthodox or Conservative Judaism (the word *church* is its equivalent)

*Tallit* — Prayer shawl worn by men during worship in the synagogue or at home

*Talmud* — Means "study"; oral traditions, discussions, and instructions in 37 volumes (English) of the great rabbis and scholars of Judaism (100 B.C.E. to 200 C.E.); consists of two distinct parts—(1) the Mishnah and a commentary on it and (2) the Gemara (there are two Gemaras, and thus two Talmuds—the Babylonian and the Palestinian); contains a commentary on Scripture written by "Tannaim" (teachers mentioned in the Mishnah, A.D. 1-200); "Amoraim" (teachers mentioned in the Gemara); and "Saborim" (reasoners who added comments to the Talmud in the sixth and seventh centuries); consists of 63 tractates. By the time the Mishnah was completed, this system of comments had become more important than the Scripture upon which it was based—thus began Talmudic or Rabbinic Judaism, culminating in what we call Orthodox Judaism; translations available in Hebrew, English, German, and possibly other languages.

*Talmud Torah* — Community religious school teaching Hebrew, Talmud, the Law (Torah), and sometimes secular subjects

*Tefillin* — Leather boxes attached to leather thongs wound around the head and arm, used by very religious Jews during prayer; the box contains portions of the Torah (Deuteronomy 6:8), also called *Phylacteries*

58

*Temple* — Place of worship of Reform Jews

*Tenach (TeNaK)* — Torah, Nevi'im, Ketuvim (the Old Testament); commentary on the Tenach called the *Oral Tradition*

*Torah* — The five books of Moses; the Law; also known as the *Chumash*

*Trefeh* — Unclean, forbidden food

*Tzaddik* — Means "righteous one"; usually applied to a spiritual leader or to one who is learned and pious

*Tzitzit* — The fringes attached to the four corners of the *tallit* (Numbers 15:38-40)

*Yahrzeit* — Death anniversary; the tombstone unveiling ceremony conducted on the first anniversary of death; each year observance of the anniversary is made at home, by the lighting of a special candle, and at synagogue

*Yarmulkah* — Skull cap used to cover men's heads, especially during worship in the synagogue or home (or *kippot*— "covering")

*Yeshivah* — Religious school of higher learning (high school, and so forth)

*Yitzkor* — Means "May he remember"; memorial to the dead and rededication to the spiritual heritage of the Fathers

## Miscellaneous

*Adonai* — Means "Lord"; no Hebrew word for the word *God* is used by Jews; the term *Ha Shem* ("the Name") is used instead (the word *God* is considered too holy)

*Aliyah* — Means "going up"; making a first visit to Eretz Yisrael; a pilgrimage

59

*Ashkenazi* — Jewish person from Central or Western European origin (Poland, Russia, Germany, France, and so forth)

*B'nai B'rith* — Means "sons of the covenant"; a Jewish fraternal organization founded in 1843

*Chasidism* — *See* Hasidism

*Eretz Yisrael* — Land of Israel

*Goy* — Nation or Gentile; *goyim* (plural)

*Ha Shem* — Means "the Name"; *see* Adonai

*Hasid* — *Hasidim* (plural); means "pious one"; follower of Hasidism

*Hasidism* — Jewish sect of the second century B.C. opposed to Hellenism and devoted to the strict observance of ritual law; also Jewish mystical sect founded in Poland about 1750 in opposition to rationalism and ritual laxity

*Meshiach* — "Anointed One"; Messiah

*Meshumad* — An apostate Jew, especially one who "converts" to "Christianity"

*"Mogam Ha Tikvah"* — Means "the hope"; Israel's national anthem

*Mogen David* — Means "shield of David"; six-pointed star commonly worn by Jews and used as a symbol of the Jewish people

*Sephardi* — Jewish person from Eastern, Oriental, or Southern Mediterranean origin (Turkey, Spain, Egypt, and so forth)

*Zion* — Israel

*Zionist* — A supporter of the idea of a Jewish state, namely, Israel

# Reading Recommendations from Our Staff

## Understanding Jewish People and Theology

Driver, S. R., and A. D. Neubauer. *The Fifty-Third Chapter of Isaiah According to the Jewish Interpreters.* Hoboken, N.J.: Ktav Publishing House, 1877.

Ebban, Abba. *My People.* New York: Random House, 1968. A history of the Jews, written as an epic drama. Excellent photographs.

Menkus, Belden, ed. *Meet the American Jew.* Nashville, Tenn.: Broadman Press, 1963. Compiled primarily for Christians by Jews for the Southern Baptist Church. Very basic, but useful.

Potok, Chaim. *The Beginning.* New York: Alfred A. Knopf, 1975.

―――. *The Chosen.* New York: Fawcett Crest, 1978. Written by a rabbi who is editor of the Jewish Publication Society of America. An attempt to describe Chasidic and Orthodox Judaism in the form of a novel. Provides the reader with a feeling for the subject—makes Chasidism, especially, more understandable. 350 pages.

―――. *The Promise.* New York: Fawcett Crest, 1986. Same description as for *The Chosen.* 350 pages.

Steinberg, Milton. *Basic Judaism.* New York: Harcourt Brace Jovanovich, 1965.

Waskow, Arthur. *Seasons of Our Joy: A Handbook of Jewish Festivals.* New York: Bantam Books, 1982.

Wouk, Herman. *This Is My God.* Garden City, N.Y.: Doubleday, 1961. A personal exploration of the Jewish relationship to, and understanding of, God.

### Jewish History

Dimont, Max. *The Jews, God, and History.* New York: Signet Books, 1962. A very basic history but well written and interesting. Good index. 421 pages.

Johnson, Paul. *A History of the Jews.* New York: Harper and Row, 1987.

### Anti-Semitism

Flannery, Edward H. *The Anguish of the Jews: Twenty-Six Centuries of Anti-Semitism* (rev. ed.). Mahwah, N.J.: Paulist Press, 1985.

Gade, Richard E. *A Historical Survey of Anti-Semitism.* Grand Rapids, Mich.: Baker Book House, n.d.

### Witnessing

Goldberg, Louis. *Our Jewish Friends* (rev. ed.). Neptune, N.J.: Loizeaux Brothers, 1983.

### Messianic Philosophy

Fruchtenbaum, Arnold. *Hebrew Christianity: Its Theology, History, and Philosophy.* Grand Rapids, Mich.: Baker Book House, 1974.

―――. *Jesus Was a Jew.* Tustin, Calif.: Ariel Press, 1981.

Fuchs, Daniel. *Israel's Holy Days.* Neptune, N.J.: Loizeaux Brothers, 1987.

Jocz, Jacob. *The Jewish People and Jesus Christ.* Grand Rapids, Mich.: Baker Book House, 1979. A leading theologian examines the problem of the Jewish people with the person and theological implications of Jesus and His ministry, and so forth.

Kac, Arthur. *The Death and Resurrection of Israel.* Grand Rapids, Mich.: Baker Book House, 1969. A sequel to *The Rebirth of the State of Israel.* Highly recommended.

―――. *The Messianic Hope.* Grand Rapids, Mich.: Baker Book House, 1975.

## Messianic Discipleship

Bell, John. *How to Be Like the Messiah: Walking the New Halakhah.* Charlotte, N.C.: Chosen People Ministries, 1987.

Maass, Eliezer. *Stand Firm.* Lansing, Ill.: American Messianic Fellowship, 1990.

## Testimonies

Frydland, Rachmiel. *When Being Jewish Was a Crime.* Cincinnati, Ohio: Messianic Literature Outreach, 1978.

Telchin, Stan. *Betrayed.* Grand Rapids, Mich.: Zondervan, 1981. A sensitive account of a loving family caught on divergent prongs of a tragic and historical conflict.

Urbach, Eliezer. *Out of the Fury.* Denver, Colo.: Zhera Publications, 1987.

# Additional Reading

## Jewish History

Allegro, John M. *The Chosen People*. Garden City, N.Y.: Doubleday, 1972. A study of Jewish history from the exile until the Bar-Kokhba revolt (sixth century B.C. to second century A.D.). The author discusses the question: "Did the Babylonian Jew lay the foundation of anti-Semitism by originating the doctrine of the 'Chosen Race'?"

Ben-Sasson, H. H., ed. *A History of the Jewish People*. Cambridge, Mass.: Harvard Univ. Press, 1976.

Blau, Joseph L., and Salo W. Baron, eds. *The Jews of the United States, 1790-1840* (3 vols.). New York: Columbia Univ. Press, 1963. Contains materials from primary sources. Provides an understanding of the first days of Jewish experience in the United States and changes in Jewish life brought about by this experience. Includes chronological lists of documents. 955 pages.

Cohen, Shaye J. D. *From the Macabees to the Mishna*. In Wayne A. Meeks, ed., *Library of Early Christianity* (Vol. 7). Philadelphia: Westminster Press, 1987.

Elbogen, Ismar. *A Century of Jewish Life*. Jewish Publication Society of America, 1944. Written with the primary intent of bringing up to date the history in Heinrich Graetz's six-volume *History of the Jews*. Helpful bibliography. 682 pages.

Finkelstein, Louis, ed. *The Jews: Their History, Their Role in Civilization, Their Religion and Culture* (3 vols.). New York: Schocken Books, 1971. Written by the chancellor of the Jewish Theological

Seminary of America. A complete intellectual account of Jewish life and thought.

Fleming, Gerald. *Hitler and the Final Solution*. Berkeley, Calif.: Univ. of California Press, 1982.

Gilbert, Martin. *Atlas of the Holocaust.* Jerusalem: Steimatsky's Agency, 1982.

—————. *The Holocaust: A History of the Jews of Europe During the Second World War.* New York: Holt, Rinehart and Winston, 1985.

—————. *Jewish History Atlas*. New York: Macmillan, 1969.

Goldwurm, Hirsch, ed. *History of the Jewish People: The Second Temple Era*. New York: Mesorah Publications, 1983.

Golub, Jacob S. *In the Days of the Second Temple*. New York: Union of American Hebrew Congregations, 1929. Especially useful for young readers.

Graetz, Heinrich. *History of the Jews* (Originally *Geschichte der Juden von den altesten Zeiten bis auf die Gegenwart*) (6 vols.). Philadelphia: Jewish Publication Society of America, 1949. Considered by many to be the most complete of any such works. Definite, obvious bias in regard to the superiority of German culture, and so forth.

Grayzel, Solomon. *A History of the Contemporary Jew: 1900 to Present.* New York: Atheneum, 1972. Written by a past professor of Jewish history at Gratz College. Concise. Useful bibliography. 179 pages.

Hull, William L. *The Fall and Rise of Israel: The Story of the Jewish People During Their Dispersal and Regathering*. Grand Rapids, Mich.: Zondervan, 1954. An excellent discussion of the subject.

Josephus, Flavias. *The Jewish War.* Gaalya Cornfeld and Paul L. Maier, eds. Grand Rapids, Mich.: Zondervan, 1982. Newly translated edition with extensive commentary and archaeological illustrations.

—————. *The Life and Works of Josephus*. John C. Whiston, trans. Grand Rapids, Mich.: Associated Publishers and Authors, n.d. Jewish historian of the Jewish wars with Rome and so forth.

Margolis, Max L., and Alexander Marx. *A History of the Jewish*

*People*. Philadelphia: World Publishing Co., 1958. Margolis was editor-in-chief of the Bible translation published by the Jewish Publication Society. Marx was professor of history at the Jewish Theological Seminary of America. An historical account of Judaism and Judaic thought. Excellent bibliography. 737 pages.

Mitscherlich, Alexander, and Fred Mielke. *Doctors of Infamy*. Henry Schuman, 1949. The head of the German Medical Commission to Military Tribunal No. 1, Nuremberg, describes Nazi atrocities.

Morse, Arthur D. *While Six Million Died*. New York: Random House, 1968. Describes America's indifference to the Jews of the Holocaust.

Rausch, David A. *A Legacy of Hatred*. Chicago: Moody Press, 1984.

Rivkin, Ellis. *The Shaping of Jewish History*. New York: Charles Scribner's Sons, 1971. Written by a professor of Jewish history at Hebrew Union College. A radically economic approach, providing valuable insights into the Pharisaic "revolution" in Judaism especially. Provocative and thoughtful.

Roth, Cecil. *A History of the Marranos*. Philadelphia: Jewish Publication Society, 1960. Writer is professor in Jewish Studies at Oxford University, England. Comprehensive account of forced conversions of Jews in Spain, and of the converts. 375 pages.

Sachar, Abram Leon. *A History of the Jews*. New York: Alfred A. Knopf, 1964. Written by a president of Brandeis University. Good bibliography and index. Comprehensive treatment of "thirty centuries of Judaism." One of the better one-volume histories.

Sachar, Howard M. *Diaspora: An Inquiry into the Contemporary Jewish World*. New York: Harper and Row, 1985.

St. John, Robert. *Tongue of the Prophets*. North Hollywood, Calif.: Wilshire Book Co., 1952. A biography of Eliezer Ben-Yehuda, the father of modern Hebrew.

Scholem, Gershom. *Origins of the Kabbalah*. Princeton, N.J.: Princeton Univ. Press, 1987.

———. *Sabbatai Zevi: The Mystical Messiah* (Bollingen Series XCIII). Princeton, N.J.: Princeton Univ. Press, 1973.

Shenker, Israel. *Coat of Many Colors: Pages from Jewish Life*.

Garden City, N.Y.: Doubleday, 1985.

Siegel, Richard, and Carl Rheius. *The Jewish Almanac*. New York: Bantam Books, 1980. A fact-filled book on the traditions, history, religion, wisdom, and achievements of the Jewish people.

Silberman, Charles E. *A Certain People*. New York: Summit Books, 1985.

Wyman, David S. *The Abandonment of the Jews: America and the Holocaust, 1941-1945*. New York: Pantheon Books, 1984.

Zeitlin, Solomon. *The Rise and Fall of the Judean State* (2 vols.). Philadelphia: Jewish Publication Society of America, 1967. Written by the professor of Rabbinic Law and Lore at Dropsie College. An account of the political, social, economic, and religious events of the second Jewish Commonwealth.

## Modern Israeli History

Antonius, George. *The Arab Awakening*. Toms River, N.J.: Capricorn Books, 1965. The most comprehensive and important work on Arab nationalism. 412 pages.

Ben-Gurion, David. *Israel*. Tel Aviv: Sabra Books, 1972. A very personal and often autobiographical history of the nation which the author helped to create.

Bright, John. *History of Israel* (3rd ed.). Philadelphia: Westminster Press, 1981.

Collins, Larry, and Dominique LaPierre. *O Jerusalem*. New York: Simon and Schuster, 1972. Well-written account of the events of 1948 from various perspectives. 657 pages.

Gilbert, Martin. *The Arab Israeli Conflict: Its History in Maps*. London: Weidenfeld and Nicolson, 1979.

Hertzberg, Arthur, ed. *The Zionist Idea*. New York: Atheneum, 1969. History contained in introduction. Source materials from 1790s to formation of Jewish state. Contains writings of the intellectuals of Zionism. With biographies. 619 pages.

Katz, Samuel. *Battleground: Fact and Fantasy in Palestine*. New York: Bantam Books, 1973. A well-documented history of the conflict between the Arabs and Israel from 1948. Somewhat pro-Israel. 239 pages.

Luttwak, Edward, and Dan Horowitz. *The Israeli Army.* New York: Harper and Row, 1975. How was the army created in a single generation from a people who had no army for several thousand years?

Peters, Joan. *From Time Immemorial: The Origins of the Arab Jewish Conflict Over Palestine.* New York: Harper and Row, 1984.

Sachar, Howard M. *A History of Israel.* New York: Alfred A. Knopf, 1976.

Segal, Ronald. *Whose Jerusalem?* New York: Bantam Books, 1973. A discussion of the possibilities for war and peace in the Middle East, with consideration being given to the personalities involved.

Shipler, David K. *Arab and Jew: Wounded Spirits in a Promised Land.* New York: Times Books, 1986.

Silverberg, Robert. *If I Forget Thee O Jerusalem.* New York: William Morrow, 1970. Presents a complete picture of the nature and construction of the state of Israel as it relates to American Jews. 611 pages.

Weizmann, Chaim. *Trial and Error* (2 vols.). Philadelphia: Jewish Publication Society of America, 1949. Biographical account of Zionism by Israel's first president; biased, but interesting.

## Jewish Theology and Tradition

Cohen, A., ed. *The Soncino Chumash.* New York: Soncino Press, 1970. The five books of Moses with Haftorah. Hebrew text with English translation and an exposition based on classical Jewish commentaries. Good index. 1,200 pages.

*Commentary Magazine,* eds. *Condition of Jewish Belief.* Northvale, N.J.: Jason Aronson, 1989. A symposium of thought on the basic topics of Judaism from the full spectrum of the rabbinate. 280 pages.

Eisendrath, Maurice N. *Can Faith Survive?* New York: McGraw-Hill, 1964. Written by a president of the Union of American Hebrew Congregations and leader of Reform Jewry. A redefinition of Jewish values and a rededication to them. Interesting.

Ganzfried, Solomon. *Kitzur Schulchan Aruch (Code of Jewish Law).* New York: Hebrew Publishing, 1961. A compilation of the rules and precepts which have governed Jewish life for centuries. Detailed. A final authority on matters of Jewish law and custom. Invaluable for understanding of Jewish tradition and orthodoxy. 562 pages.

Gaster, Theodore H. *Festivals of the Jewish Year: A Modern Interpretation and Guide.* New York: William Morrow, 1953.

Glazer, Nathan. *American Judaism* (2nd ed.). Chicago: Univ. of Chicago Press, 1972. Written by a professor of Sociology at University of California, Berkeley. Concerns Jewish identity, immigration to the United States, and the outlook of Jews today with regard to social and religious needs. 149 pages.

Herberg, Will. *Judaism and the Modern Man.* Philadelphia: Jewish Publication Society of America, 1959. Discusses the question: "How relevant is Judaism to life today?" 310 pages.

Heschel, Abraham. *The Sabbath.* New York: Farrar, Straus and Giroux, 1975.

Idelsohn, A. Z. *Jewish Liturgy.* New York: Schocken Books, 1932. An excellent resource for a study of ritual, music, and liturgy in Judaism by a scholar in this field.

Jacobs, Louis. *Principles of the Jewish Faith.* Northvale, N.J.: Jason Aronson, 1988.

Kaplan, Mordecai M. *Judaism as a Civilization.* New York: Schocken Books, 1967. Reconstructionist Judaism discussed by its founder. 522 pages.

————. *The Meaning of God in Modern Jewish Religion.* Reconstructionist Press, 1962. Interpretation of Reconstructionism. 368 pages.

Kertzer, Morris N. *What Is a Jew?* New York: Macmillan, 1960. Written by the rabbi of a large temple in New York state. A brief account of the religious practices of the reform tradition of Judaism. 179 pages.

Kitov, A. E. *The Jew and His Home.* New York: Shengold Publishers, 1973. A very informative description of the traditional view of daily life in a Jewish home.

Kolatch, Alfred J. *Who's Who in the Talmud.* New York: Jonathan David Publishers, 1964.

Landman, Isaac, ed. *The Universal Jewish Encyclopedia* (10 vols.). University Jewish Encyclopedia Co., 1948. An excellent source of information for those who desire extensive materials.

Landman, L., ed. *Messianism in the Talmudic Era*. Hoboken, N.J.: Ktav Publishing House, 1979.

Levi, Isaac. *The Synagogue: Its History and Function*. London: Valentine Mitchell, 1963.

Moore, George Foot. *Judaism in the First Centuries of the Christian Era* (3 vols.). Cambridge, Mass.: Cambridge Univ. Press, 1948. Written by a non-Jewish Harvard University professor of the history of religion. Offers considerable depth of information on the subject of Rabbinic Judaism and the Talmud and is considered perhaps the best work of its kind.

Rabinowicz, Rabbi Tzvi. *A Guide to Life: Jewish Laws and Customs of Mourning*. Northvale, N.J.: Jason Aronson, 1989.

Sandmel, Samuel. *We Jews and Jesus*. New York: Oxford Univ. Press, 1965. Written by professor of Bible and Hellenistic Literature at Hebrew Union College. A review of Jewish attitudes toward Jesus and Christianity with explanations from an historical perspective. 153 pages.

Schauss, Hayyim. *The Jewish Festivals from Their Beginnings to Our Own Day*. New York: Union of American Hebrew Congregations, 1965.

Shulman, Albert M. *Gateway to Judaism* (2 vols.). New York: Thomas Yoseloff Publishers, 1971. Concise encyclopedia of Jewish thought and life (including doctrines of Judaism, ceremonies, literature, and so forth). Written in a readable form and organized and divided into chapters. Obviously not comprehensive, but useful for those not desirous of obtaining a more extensive work.

Siegel, Richard; Michael Strassfeld; and Sharon Strassfeld. *The First Jewish Catalog*. Philadelphia: Jewish Publication Society of America, 1973.

Sloti, Judah J., ed. *The Soncino Talmud* (18 vols.). London: Soncino Press, 1952.

Strassfeld, Michael. *The Jewish Holidays: A Guide and Commentary*. New York: Harper and Row, 1985.

Syme, Daniel P. *The Jewish Home: A Guide for Jewish Living*. Northvale, N.J.: Jason Aronson, 1989.

Weiner, Herbert. *9½ Mystics*. New York: Macmillan/ Collier Books, 1969. An interesting "modern" account of Jewish mysticism.

Wiesel, Elie. *Souls on Fire*. New York: Random House, 1972. Biographical sketches and legendary accounts of Chasidic masters.

*Zohar, The*. Harry Sperling and Maurice Simon, trans. London: Soncino Press, 1933. A form of commentary on the mystical meaning of the Pentateuch. Originally written in Aramaic and Hebrew. Purportedly written by Rabbi Simeon ben Yohai, second century A.D.

### Jewish Literature

Aleichem, Sholom. *Collected Stories of Sholom Aleichem* (2 vols.). New York: Crown Publishers, 1946. Stories of the Old Country which have become part of Jewish culture. "Fiddler on the Roof" is taken from this collection. Glossary. 689 pages.

Ausubel, Nathan, ed. *A Treasury of Jewish Folklore*. New York: Crown Publishers, 1948. For an understanding of Jewish tradition, superstition, and folk culture, this is invaluable. Glossary. 734 pages.

―――. *A Treasury of Jewish Humor*. New York: Paperback Library, 1967. Interesting and enjoyable—the flavor of Jewish culture. 760 pages.

Bellow, Saul, ed. *Great Jewish Short Stories*. Laurel, Md.: Dell Publications, 1963. A collection of stories from Europe and America. 414 pages.

Feuer, Leon I. *Jewish Literature Since the Bible* (2 vols.). New York: Union of American Hebrew Congregations, 1937. A collection of Jewish writings from the "Apocrypha."

Glatzer, Nahum N., ed. *Hammer on the Rock: A Midrash Reader Wisdom and Poetry of the Talmud and Midrash*. New York: Schocken Books, 1975.

Golden, Harry. *You're Entitle*. Greenwich, Conn.: Fawcett Press, 1962. Other volumes by author are *Enjoy, Enjoy; Only in America; For 2 Cents Plain*. A leading Jewish humorist writes about Jewish life and experience in the United States.

Greenburg, Sidney. *A Modern Treasury of Jewish Thought*. New

York: Thomas Yoseloff Publishers, 1960.

Keston, Hermann, ed. *Heinrich Heine: Works of Prose.* New York: L. B. Fisher, 1943.

Lewis, Sinclair. *It Can't Happen Here.* Garden City, N.Y.: Doubleday, 1935. As the events in Germany confronted the world, Americans declared that mass murder, death chambers, and the nightmare which Hitler created could never take place in our "free" society. Lewis relates American temperament and culture to that of Germans and, in this novel, poses interesting questions.

Michener, James A. *The Source.* New York: Fawcett Crest, 1984. A novel-form "history of Israel" using archaeology to move the setting from one period to the next. Many inaccuracies.

Nahmad, H. M., ed. *A Portion in Paradise and Other Jewish Folktales.* New York: Schocken Books, 1974. Fascinating legends, and so forth.

Newman, Louis. *The Hasidic Anthology.* Northvale, N.J.: Jason Aronson, 1987.

Potok, Chaim. *My Name Is Asher Lev.* New York: Fawcett Crest, 1972. Same description as for *The Chosen.* 350 pages.

Rosten, Leo. *The Joys of Yiddish.* New York: Pocket Books, 1970.

————. *Treasury of Jewish Quotations.* New York: McGraw-Hill, 1972.

Steinsaltz, Adin. *The Essential Talmud.* New York: Basic Books, 1976.

Uris, Leon. *Exodus.* New York: Bantam Books, 1959. Novel which offers an excellent picture of the years leading up to 1948 and of the kind of people involved in the Jews' struggle.

Vilnay, Zev. *Legends of Jerusalem.* Philadelphia: Jewish Publication Society of America, 1977.

————. *Legends of Judea and Samaria.* Philadelphia: Jewish Publication Society of America, 1977.

Waxman, Meyer. *History of Jewish Literature: From the Close of the Bible to Our Own Day.* New York: Block Publishing, 1936.

## Archaeology

Albright, W. F. *The Archeology of Palestine*. New York: Pelican, 1949. An archaeological survey of the peoples and cultures of this area. Albright was one of the world's leading archaeologists.

Baez-Camargo, Goncalo. *Archaeological Commentary on the Bible*. Garden City, N.Y.: Doubleday/Galilee Books, 1986.

Baney, Ralph E. *Search for Sodom and Gomorrah*. Hortonville, Wisc.: CAM Press, 1962. Interesting facts about the Dead Sea.

Ben-Dov, Meir. *In the Shadow of the Temple: The Discovery of Ancient Jerusalem*. New York: Harper and Row, 1982.

Bowen, Barbara M. *Through Bowen Museum with Bible in Hand*. Grand Rapids, Mich.: Eerdmans, 1946. Offers archaeology facts which explain many Biblical expressions and Israelite customs.

Burrows, Millar. *The Dead Sea Scrolls*. New York: Viking, 1955. An account of the most important archaeological discovery of modern times, with "translations of the principal scrolls and a study of their contributions to our understanding of Biblical times." Author was a Yale professor.

Cross, Frank Moore, Jr. *The Ancient Library of Qumran*. Garden City, N.Y.: Doubleday/Anchor Books, 1961. Author is considered to be a top authority in this field. "A comprehensive study of the Dead Sea Scrolls and the community which owned them." An up-to-date survey. Very readable. 243 pages.

Davis, George T. B. *Bible Prophecies Fulfilled Today*. New York: Million Testaments Campaigns, 1951. Good background material.

————. *Fulfilled Prophecies That Prove the Bible*. New York: Million Testaments Campaigns, 1931. Good background material.

Finegan, Jack. *Light from the Ancient Past*. Princeton, N.J.: Princeton Univ. Press, 1949. Archaeological background of Judaism (and Christianity). Very useful.

Free, Joseph P. *Archeology and Bible History*. Wheaton, Ill.: Scripture Press, 1972. Biblical criticism answered and explained by archaeological discoveries.

Jidejian, Nina. *Tyre Through the Ages*. Dar El-Mashreq, 1969.

Excellent description of Tyre, Sidon, and other ancient cities.

Layard, Austen. *Discoveries Among the Ruins of Ninevah and Babylon.* New York: Harper and Brothers, 1853. An interesting account of the archaeological findings in these two ancient capitals.

Mare, Harold W. *Archaeology of the Jerusalem Area.* Grand Rapids, Mich.: Baker Book House, 1987.

Robinson, George L. *Sarcophagus of an Ancient Civilization.* New York: Macmillan, 1930. History and archaeological material on such places as Petra, Edom, and Israel. Excellent.

Wright, Thomas. *Early Travels in Palestine.* Henry G. Bohn, 1948.

Yadin, Yigael. *Bar-Kokhba: The Rediscovery of the Legendary Hero of the Second Jewish Revolt Against Rome.* New York: Random House, 1971. Archaeological account of the second Jewish revolt against Rome and its leader, Bar-Kokhba. Based on discoveries by the author (Israel's leading archaeologist) made in the early 1970s.

―――. *Hazor: The Rediscovery of the Great Citadel of the Bible.* New York: Random House, 1975.

―――. *Masada: Herod's Fortress and the Zealots Last Stand.* New York: Random House, 1966. Masada archaeological expedition, Hebrew University, Jerusalem. Has excellent pictures of the archaeological work at Masada, the last holdout of the Jewish people against the Romans.

―――. *The Temple Scroll.* London: Weidenfeld and Nicholson, 1985.

### Jewish Philosophy

Agus, J. B. *The Evolution of Jewish Thought.* New York: Harper and Row/Abelard-Schuman, 1959.

Buber, Martin. *Kingship of God.* New York: Harper and Rowe, 1967.

―――. *Moses: The Revelation and the Covenant.* New York: Harper and Brothers, 1958.

Heschel, Abraham. *Between Man and God.* New York: Harper and Brothers, 1959.

————. *Man Is Not Alone*. Farrar, Strauss and Giroux. 1952.

————. *Man's Quest for God*. New York: Charles Scribner's Sons, 1954.

Maimonides, Moses. *Guide for the Perplexed*. M. Friedlander, trans. London: Pardes Publishing House, 1904. Maimonides is one of the two most significant Jewish philosophers and theologians of the Medieval Period. His spiritual wisdom has been appreciated by Jews and non-Jews alike.

————. *Mishnah Torah*. Philip Birnbaum, ed. New York: Hebrew Publishing, 1967.

Mendelssohn, Moses. *Jerusalem: And Other Jewish Writings*. New York: Schocken Books, 1969. Mendelssohn, grandfather of composer Felix Mendelssohn, was a remarkable man and a scholar of great culture. He was held in high esteem by the most important people of his day and contributed much to the eventual emancipation of the Jewish people in Germany.

Runes, Dagobert D., ed. *The Hebrew Impact on Western Civilization*. New York: Philosophical Library, 1951. Offers a comprehensive and factual account of the Jewish contributions to Western culture and society. 875 pages.

Yaffe, James. *The American Jews: Portrait of a Split Personality*. New York: Random House, 1968.

## Judeo-Christian Relations

Baeck, Leo. *Judaism and Christianity*. Philadelphia: Jewish Publication Society of America, 1958.

Borowitz, Eugene B. *Contemporary Christologies: A Jewish Response*. Mahwah, N.J.: Paulist Press, 1980.

Bruce, F. F. *Israel and the Nations from the Exodus to the Fall of the Second Temple*. Grand Rapids, Mich.: Eerdmans, 1963. An interesting account by a Bible scholar.

Danielou, Jean. *The Theology of Jewish Christianity: The Development of Christian Doctrine Before the Council of Nicaea* (Vol. 1). John A. Baker, trans. London: Darten Longman and Todd; Chicago: Henry Regnery, 1964.

Davies, William David. *Christian Origin and Judaism.* Philadelphia: Westminster Press, 1962. A serious and scholarly examination of this timely subject.

Duvernoy, Claude. *Controversy of Zion.* Green Forest, Ark.: New Leaf Press, 1987.

Eckstein, Rabbi Yechiel. *What Christians Should Know About Jews and Judaism.* Waco, Tex.: Word Publishing, 1984.

Ellis, E. Earle. *Paul's Use of the Old Testament.* Grand Rapids, Mich.: Baker Book House, 1981.

Hagner, Donald. *The Jewish Reclamation of Jesus.* Grand Rapids, Mich.: Zondervan/Academic Books, 1984.

Isaac, Jules. *The Teaching of Contempt: Christian Roots of Anti-Semitism.* New York: Holt, Rinehart and Winston, 1964.

Katz, Jacob. *Exclusiveness and Tolerance.* New York: Oxford Univ. Press, 1961. A unique discussion of Jewish-Christian relations in Medieval and modern times.

Lachs, Samuel Tobias. *A Rabbinic Commentary on the New Testament.* Hoboken, N.J.: Ktav Publishing House, 1987.

Lapide, Pinchas E. *Hebrew in the Church: The Foundations of Jewish-Christian Dialogue.* Grand Rapids, Mich.: Eerdmans, 1984.

————. *The Resurrection of Jesus: A Jewish Perspective.* Minneapolis, Minn.: Augsburg Publishing House, 1983.

Lapide, Pinchas E., and Ulrich Luz. *Jesus in Two Perspectives: A Jewish-Christian Dialogue.* Minneapolis, Minn.: Augsburg Publishing House, 1979.

Lapide, Pinchas E., and Jurgen Moltmann. *Jewish Monotheism and Christian Trinitarian Doctrine: A Dialogue by Pinchas Lapide and Jurgen Moltmann.* Philadelphia: Fortress Press, 1979.

Lapide, Pinchas E., and Peter Stuhlmacher. *Paul Rabbi and Apostle.* Minneapolis, Minn.: Augsburg Publishing House, 1984.

Limburg, James. *Judaism: An Introduction for Christians.* Minneapolis, Minn.: Augsburg Publishing House, 1987.

Moshe, Beth. *Judaism's Truth Answers the Missionaries.* New York: Bloch Publishing, 1987.

Newman, Louis I. *The Jewish People, Faith and Life: A Guide*

*Book and Manual of Information Concerning Jewry and Judaism.* New York: Bloch Publishing, 1964.

Parkes, James William. *Judaism and Christianity.* Chicago: Univ. of Chicago Press, 1948.

————. *The Conflict of the Church and the Synagogue.* New York: New American Library/Meridian Books, 1961.

Pragai, Michael J. *Faith and Fulfillment: Christians and the Return to the Promised Land.* London: Valentine Mitchell, 1985.

Pruter, Carl. *Jewish Christians in the United States: A Bibliography.* New York: Garland Publishing, 1987.

Rudin, A. James. *Israel for Christians: Understanding Modern Israel.* Philadelphia: Fortress Press, 1983.

Runes, Dagobert B. *The Jew and the Cross.* New York: Philosophical Library, 1965.

Shermis, Michael. *Jewish Christian Relations: An Annotated Bibliography and Resource Guide.* Bloomington: Indiana Univ. Press, 1988.

Siegel, Gerald. *The Jew and the Christian Missionary: A Jewish Response to Missionary Christianity.* New York: Cataw Publishing House, 1981.

Stern, David H. *Messianic Jewish Manifesto.* Jerusalem: Jewish New Testament Publications, 1988.

Tannenbaum, Mark H.; Marvin R. Wilson; and James A. Rudin, eds. *Evangelicals and Jews in an Age of Pluralism.* Grand Rapids, Mich.: Baker Book House, 1984.

————. *Evangelicals and Jews in Conversation.* Grand Rapids, Mich.: Baker Book House, 1978.

————. *A Time to Speak.* Grand Rapids, Mich.: Baker Book House, 1987.

Wilson, Marvin R. *Our Father Abraham: Jewish Roots of the Christian Faith.* Grand Rapids, Mich.: Eerdmans, 1989.

**Works by Jewish Believers**

Edersheim, Alfred. *Sketches of Jewish Social Life in the Days of Christ.* Religious Tract Society, 1908. An authoritative study calculated to enlighten the serious Bible student. (Edersheim also authored the definitive work: *Life and Times of Jesus the Messiah*, Eerdmans, 1972.)

Feinberg, Charles. *Israel at the Center of History and Revelation.* Portland, Ore.: Multnomah Press, 1980.

――――. *Israel in the Light of Prophecy.* Chicago: Moody Press, 1964. A modern Hebrew-Christian scholar examines Israel's destiny from a prophetic perspective.

Gartenhaus, Jacob. *Christ Killers, Past and Present.* Chattanooga: Tenn.: Hebrew Christian Press, 1975.

――――. *Famous Hebrew Christians.* Chattanooga, Tenn.: International Board of Jewish Missions, 1979.

――――. *The Spiritual History of Israel.* London: Eyre and Spotiswode, 1961.

Kac, Arthur. *The Rebirth of the State of Israel.* Grand Rapids, Mich.: Baker Book House, 1958. An excellent study of the Biblical background and Scriptural implications of the reestablishment of the state of Israel.

Koser, Hilda. *Come and Get It.* Orlando, Fla.: Golden Rule Book Press, 1987.

Reich, Max I. *The Messianic Hope of Israel.* Chicago: Moody Press, 1945.

Rubin, Barry. *You Bring the Bagels, I'll Bring the Gospel.* Old Tappan, N.J.: Fleming H. Revell, 1989.

*Schonfield, Hugh Joseph. *History of Jewish Christianity from the First to the Twentieth Century.* London: Gerald Duckworth, 1936.

## Messiah in Jewish Thought

Fredricks, Ernest; William S. Green; and Jacob Neusner. *Judaisms and Their Messiahs at the Turn of the Christian Era.* New York: Cambridge Univ. Press, 1987.

Greenstone, Julius H. *The Messiah Idea in Jewish History.* Philadelphia: Jewish Publication Society of America, 1906.

*At the time H. J. Schonfield wrote this text, he claimed to be a believer in Jesus as the Messiah. This is no longer true.

Klausner, Joseph. *The Messianic Idea in Israel.* New York: Macmillan, 1955.

Patai, Raphael. *The Messiah Texts: Jewish Legends of Three Thousand Years.* Detroit: Wayne State University Press, 1979.

Scholem, Gershom. *The Messianic Idea in Judaism and Other Essays on Jewish Spirituality.* New York: Schocken Books, 1987.

Serachek, Joseph. *The Doctrine of the Messiah in Medieval Jewish Literature.* New York: Harmon Press, 1968.

Silver, Abba-Hillel. *A History of Messianic Speculation in Israel.* Glouchester, Mass.: Peter Smith, 1987.

# Appendix: About Chosen People Ministries

Chosen People Ministries was established by God as an instrument of the Messiah to bring the Gospel to Jewish people around the world.

## OUR BEGINNINGS

In 1894, Rabbi Leopold Cohn founded this ministry in the Brownsville section of Brooklyn, New York soon after he accepted Jesus as his Messiah. He began the mission by holding Gospel meetings in a store front facility that previously was a horse stable. From humble beginnings, the mission started by God through Rabbi Cohn grew to be a worldwide effort, dedicated to reaching Jewish people with the Gospel.

The foundation of his work for the Lord was grounded in Romans 1:16,"For I am not ashamed of the Gospel of Christ: for it is the power of God unto salvation to every one that believeth; to the Jew first, and also to the Greek" (KJV).

## OUR MINISTRIES

It is our specific ministry to preach the Gospel of Jesus the Messiah, and to show our Lord's love to the Jewish people throughout the world.

Chosen People Ministries continues to evangelize and disciple Jewish people around the world through the most effective and creative ways possible. Our representatives continue to do one-on-one evangelistic work, hold worship services, fellowship meetings, Bible studies, and plant congregations in many areas around the world including North America, Israel, Europe, South America and the former Soviet Union. Personal evangelism is accomplished through various methods, such as personal visitation, telephone calls and sharing door-to-door.

By helping local churches relate to the Jewish people, we greatly increase their effectiveness in witnessing. Special presentations, such as *Messiah in the Passover*, inform Christians of the significance of studying the Bible from a Jewish perspective. And our *Jewish Evangelism Seminars* help bridge the gap that sometimes exists between the church and the Jewish community.

During the Jewish holidays, we utilize diverse forms of media to further advance the Gospel to both the Jewish and Gentile communities. For example, we air television programs that provide a witness to the Jewish community as well as insight and instruction to Christians. Topics include *Passover* and *The Day of Atonement*.

Our monthly periodical, *The Chosen People*, keeps its readers abreast of the world of Jewish missions.

Chosen People Ministries also provides ministry to children and teenagers: all of our branches have Bible classes, and a special camping program is conducted each year.

There are many exciting volunteer programs available for those who desire direct involvement with Chosen People Ministries. One is through our Summer Training and Evangelism Program (STEP) which, through specialized classes, prepares each member to share his or her faith with Jewish people. Teams have ministered in such places as New York, Chicago, Toronto, Paris and Berlin. Our Volunteer Involvement Program (VIP) provides a way for Christians to reach out to their local Jewish communities.

## OUR BELIEFS

All workers and Board members of Chosen People Ministries must subscribe to doctrines fundamental to the faith. We declare and affirm our belief in the following:

- The Divine inspiration, inerrancy, and authority of both the Old and New Testaments.
- The triune God, and the death of the Lord Jesus as the only begotten Son of God and the promised Messiah.
- Messiah's sacrificial blood atonement at Calvary, His bodily resurrection from the dead, and His second coming.

## SEE THE BIBLE THROUGH JEWISH EYES

Our workers are available to share fascinating Old Testament Biblical insights with your congregation or home group. Towards this end, Chosen People Ministries has developed an exciting presentation: *Messiah in the Passover. Messiah in the Passover* is more than a sermon. Our representative sets a Passover table with the traditional Jewish symbols and explains the links between the Seder and the Last Supper—all pointing toward Jesus, the Lamb of God who takes away the sins of the world. This unique message adds new meaning to the communion service. Another interesting message is *The Fall Feasts of Israel*, a presentation that shows how the holiest days of the Jewish year point to Jesus. Our staff members also enjoy speaking on other topics which highlight the Jewish roots of our Christian faith.

## SEE ISRAEL THROUGH JEWISH EYES

Once you tour the Holy Land with Chosen People Ministries, the Scriptures you love will be transformed. But it's not the Bible that changes—it's you! Your feet, your hands, your eyes—not to mention your heart—will follow the course of Biblical history from the Old Testament to the New. Join one of our tours to Israel and "See Israel through Jewish Eyes!"

## INTERNET OUTREACH

Chosen People Ministries maintains a dynamic evangelistic web page at www.chosenpeople.com containing personal testimonies, Messianic prophecies, and answers to common Jewish objections. The web page also has an informative section where Christians can learn more about the Jewish heritage of their faith as well as how to witness to their Jewish friends, and order Messianic materials through our online store.

## OUR PROMISE TO YOU

As gifts are received from our supporters, we will strive to be faithful stewards not only of our finances, but also with the time and talents God has given us. Gifts indicated for a particular missionary or evangelistic endeavor will be allocated as requested.

As a supporter of our ministry, you will receive our monthly publication, *The Chosen People*. You will also receive a monthly prayer letter giving you the opportunity to contribute to a particular worker or project.

As a charter member of the ECFA (Evangelical Council for Financial Accountability), we are committed to having outside auditors publish our financial statement. In Canada, we are members of the CCCC (Canadian Council of Christian Charities), the Canadian counterpart of the ECFA. Upon request, you may receive a copy of their statement and full financial disclosure.

# Tools for the Harvest

*The field of Jewish evangelism is ripe with hearts waiting for the word of salvation. On the next few pages are some of our favorite tools for helping you in the harvest.*

### HOW TO INTRODUCE YOUR JEWISH FRIENDS TO THE MESSIAH—

This guide gives a helpful overview of Judaism (past and present) as well as an understanding of God's plan for the Jewish people. Easy to understand sections on Messianic prophecy and prophecy concerning Israel, as well as a deeper look at objections you are most likely to hear from a Jewish person make this a book every Christian who cares about witnessing should have. *(#3004) $6.95*

### WITNESSING PAK—Contains nine

tracts that are perfect for reading and sharing. Complete with its own tract wallet, the Witnessing Pak includes practical how-to's of Jewish evangelism, and tracts containing persuasive proofs that show Jesus is the long-awaited Messiah. *(#2020) $2.95*

### IS IT REASONABLE TO BE JEWISH AND BELIEVE IN JESUS?—This

excellent witnessing tool to give to your Jewish friend contains short testimonies of fifteen Jewish believers in Jesus, as well as a list of Messianic prophecies and a challenge to consider Yeshua (Jesus) as the promised Messiah of Israel. *(#2025) $2.95*

### HOW TO BE LIKE THE MESSIAH—Written

especially to help Jewish believers in their new walk with the Messiah, chapters include Telling your Family, Raising Jewish Children, Messianic Lifestyles, and more.

*(#3015) $9.95*

### VIDEO TAPE OF RUSSIAN TESTIMONIES—Do you know a

Russian Jewish person who is interested in spiritual things? This video tape contains the testimonies of five Russian Jewish immigrants who came to this country looking for freedom, and found true freedom in Jesus, the Messiah. *(#8017) $14.95*

*See last page for ordering instructions.*

Passover is always a joy as the Jewish family gathers to celebrate family traditions and the historic release of the Jewish people from bondage in Egypt.

This video presents the Passover in a sensitive and relevant way, and clearly shows that Yeshua (Jesus) is the Messiah of Israel. Set around a realistic Passover family dinner, the Seder ceremony is reenacted, focusing in detail on the meaning of each of the ancient rituals the Jewish people have been practicing for over three thousand years.

*Messiah in the Passover* vividly portrays the unique symbolic and spiritual significance of this feast and presents thought-provoking insight for both Jews and Gentiles.

*(#8006) $14.95*

*"If only my family could have seen Passover like this…"*

CHOSEN PEOPLE MINISTRIES PRESENTS

M ESSIAH IN THE PASSOVER

*See last page for ordering instructions.*

# Messianic books . . .

## Israel's Glorious Future—
As the nation of Israel struggles to regain control of the land . . . as the nations fight and riot against her . . . . How can we know that Israel's future will indeed be glorious? By exploring the ancient prophecies, this book reveals the faithfulness of God to the everlasting covenants. *(#3038) $7.95*

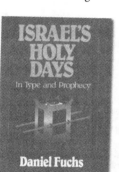

## Daniel: God's Man in Babylon—
See how the Book of Daniel applies to our situation today—and tomorrow. Finally, here's a uniquely Jewish perspective that sheds new light on the events of Revelation, from God's plan for Israel to Messianic prophecy. *(#3028) $12.95*

## Israel's Holy Days—
The more one studies the Bible, both Old and New Testaments, the more one realizes that Leviticus 23 is more than a list of holy days; it is actually an outline of God's calendar from eternity to eternity. The author examines the festivals, their history, present celebration in the synagogue and home, and their prophetic fulfillment. *(#3013) $4.95*

## The Fall Feasts of Israel—
This book will help you understand three of Israel's most significant festivals: *Rosh Hashanah, Yom Kippur* and *Sukkot.* A complete examination of each feast includes a look at its Biblical institution, its celebration in the time of Christ, and its observance by Jewish people today. *(#3042) $11.95*

## Out of the Fury—
Have you ever asked, "Where was God during the Holocaust?" From the ravages of war-torn Europe to the turmoil of an emerging Israel, retired Chosen People Ministries worker Eliezer Urbach relates his incredible odyssey. Driven from Poland and orphaned by the Nazis, Eliezer faced hunger, persecution and despair before realizing that he was caught in a world that held answers only in the Person of Jesus, the Messiah. *(#3017) $6.95*

*See last page for ordering instructions.*

# and music . . .

**Shalom Jerusalem—**
**Cassette & CD:** Recorded live in the City of David, this music weaves the purity of worship into the fabric of Messianic praise. Rich and deep as the history of Jerusalem.
**Video:** Words seem inadequate as you experience God's faithfulness to the nation of Israel and see a glimpse of her glorious destiny.
*Cassette: (#4022) $9.95*
*CD: (#4021) $15.95*
*Video: (#8014) $19.95*

**HaMoedim: The Festivals of God—**
Steve McConnell's album shines with exquisite melodies. These songs are being sung in Messianic congregations throughout the world. It is a celebration of life worthy of the Master.
*Cassette: (#4028) $10.95*
*CD: (#4027) $15.95*

**Up to Zion—**Worshipful music led by Paul Wilbur, former lead singer of Israel's Hope. *Up to Zion* is a chorus of beautiful voices and great brass and instrumental sections backed by a praising, clapping congregation. A great tape to listen to while jogging or walking!
*Cassette: (#4018) $10.95*
*CD: (#4020) $15.95*

**The Love of God—**This release by Marty Goetz features timeless songs based on God's never ending love for His people. Songs include *The Spirit of the Lord, Hineni* (Here I Am), *Psalm 23, For Zion's Sake,* and *King of the Jews.*
*Cassette: (#4005) $10.95*
*CD: (#4019) $14.95*

**Messianic Praise—**
Music from Messianic artists weaves the purity of worship into the fabric of praise. Pure joy!
*Cassette: (#4030) $10.95*
*CD: (#4029) $15.95*

*See last page for ordering instructions.*

# TO ORDER, MAIL IN THIS FORM *or* CALL 1-800-333-4936 *or* VISIT OUR ONLINE STORE AT www.chosenpeople.com

Name _____

Address _____

City _____

State/Prov. _____ Zip/PC _____

| Qty | Item | Price Each | Code | Total |
|-----|------|-----------|------|-------|
|     |      |           |      |       |
|     |      |           |      |       |
|     |      |           |      |       |
|     |      |           |      |       |
|     |      |           |      |       |

SUBTOTAL

Shipping & Handling*

*Thank you for your order!* TOTAL

## \*Standard Shipping & Handling

| $0-$10 | add $2 |
| $10.01-$20 | add $3 |
| $20.01-$30 | add $4 |
| $30.01-$50 | add $6 |
| $50.01-$100 | add $8 |
| over $100 | add $10 |

### International Orders
*Delivery charges will be billed. Please circle your preference.*

Surface Mail        Air Mail

## METHOD OF PAYMENT:

☐ Check or money order enclosed $ _____

☐ VISA  ☐ MasterCard  Credit Card # ☐☐☐☐☐☐☐☐☐☐☐☐☐☐☐☐

Expiration Date _____  Signature _____  Phone: *(in case we have questions about your order)* ( ___ ) ___

**Chosen People Ministries • 241 East 51st Street New York, NY 10022 • 1-800-333-4936 • www.chosenpeople.com**